I0487819

Sell More ... *An Entrepreneur's Guide To Marketing On A Small Budget Strategies That Make A Big Difference*

"Sell More" is a very realistic and down to earth guide to build your business. Judy used such practical and fun examples that anyone can apply her techniques to their growing venture(s). And, above all, Judy inspired the mind to use its creative side!
Paula Rizk, Franchise Owner of Pizza Pan

I work in the nonprofit arena and wasn't sure if this book would have a lot to offer in terms of usability, but I was wrong. It was easy to apply the marketing ideas in our efforts to get referrals. The customer service section fits with our direct service to youth and the entire book is applicable to the youth we serve and services we provide. As a supervisor, my favorite quote was, "Make it your job to catch people doing things right. It isn't just your employee's skillset that matters, it is their mindset." I always believed it was important to recognize and acknowledge staff's great work. Now I know why.
Wayne Bailey MA, CRT, LSW, Director of Homeless Services, Daymark, Inc.

"Sell More" is filled with a lot of practical advice ... what one might call common sense. However, as I learned early in my career, there is nothing quite as uncommon as common sense.
Michael Logan, ISA, Owner of Trace of Time, www.traceoftime.com

Judy's book, "Sell More," shows us how to sell efficiently and creatively. We all have it inside ourselves, but this book shows us how and gives us the courage to be the best. Judy is witty and intriguing and knows how to make it fun. While reading "Sell More," I was thinking, "That is a great idea!" I hadn't thought about that but I can do that. "I sell affordable housing."
Janet Henderson, Real Estate, multi-million dollar producer

"Sell More" is a must read for anyone who wants to succeed. It offers a combination of how-to and do-it-yourself solutions that confront a budding or struggling entrepreneur. Makes me wish I was much younger and had these concepts in mind, my business could have flourished to a greater degree.
Myron Abood

"Sell More" will light or re-kindle the entrepreneurial flame in all those fortunate enough to read it and open their minds to think beyond the square. As a presenter Judy is always a true motivator. She has now encapsulated her performance enhancing ability into the written word. I really enjoyed the positive way she re-enforces every point by repetition without seeming to be repetitious! In a thoughtful way Judy conveys the fact that change is good and us 'old dogs' should fully embrace the power of the internet and the new tricks we can all learn. This book is a "road map to success."
Marcus Tilley, Entrepreneur, Radio Program Host & Producer

Any reader of "Sell More" will surely want to include it as one of their top reference books, for it includes a wealth of selling, marketing and general business tips told in an upbeat, informative, easily relatable format. Ms. McKay offers up creative and timely criteria for those interested in improving their marketing skills, beginning a career in sales, or seeking ways to stay current in the ever changing marketplace. Bookmarks and highlighter highly suggested when you read this!
Nancy Foster, Director Leisure Travel Sales, St. Pete/Clearwater CVB

Sell More

✦

An Entrepreneur's Guide To Marketing On A Small Budget Strategies That Make A Big Difference

Sell More

✦

An Entrepreneur's Guide To Marketing On A Small Budget Strategies That Make A Big Difference

Judy McKay

iUniverse, Inc.
New York Lincoln Shanghai

Sell More
An Entrepreneur's Guide To Marketing On A Small Budget
Strategies That Make A Big Difference

Copyright © 2007 by Judy McKay

All rights reserved. No part of this book may be used or reproduced by any means, graphic, electronic, or mechanical, including photocopying, recording, taping or by any information storage retrieval system without the written permission of the publisher except in the case of brief quotations embodied in critical articles and reviews.

iUniverse books may be ordered through booksellers or by contacting:

iUniverse
2021 Pine Lake Road, Suite 100
Lincoln, NE 68512
www.iuniverse.com
1-800-Authors (1-800-288-4677)

Because of the dynamic nature of the Internet, any Web addresses or links contained in this book may have changed since publication and may no longer be valid.

The information, ideas, and suggestions in this book are not intended to render professional advice. Before following any suggestions contained in this book, you should consult your personal accountant or other financial advisor. Neither the author nor the publisher shall be liable or responsible for any loss or damage allegedly arising as a consequence of your use or application of any information or suggestions in this book.

ISBN: 978-0-595-46127-1 (pbk)
ISBN: 978-0-595-90428-0 (ebk)

Printed in the United States of America

This book is dedicated to everyone who dares to unleash their entrepreneurial spirit, to take a risk and create their own business.

"Twenty years from now you will be more disappointed by the things you didn't do than by the ones you did. So throw off the bowlines. Sail away from the safe harbor. Catch the tradewinds in your sails. Explore. Dream. Discover."
Mark Twain

Contents

Introduction

✦

You are the daredevil, the dreamer, the explorer, the risk taker of the 21st Century. You are an entrepreneur!

Congratulations! You dared to believe in possibilities. While other people dream, you took action. You didn't just talk about starting your own business. You had the courage to leave what had, in the past, been viewed as the safe career path.

Despite the cautions of family and friends, statistics that illustrate more small businesses fail than succeed, despite it all, *you became an entrepreneur.*

Many entrepreneurs started their businesses because they felt suffocated by rules, corporate politics, lack of recognition, favoritism, and unfair compensation. They felt frustrated and stifled. Their contributions did more to fill their employer's pockets then their own. Why did you take the leap? Was it by choice or out of necessity? Sometimes in life you need to take a calculated risk and go against the odds.

Business success requires vision, focus, discipline, leadership, confidence and the drive to achieve. Like today's entrepreneurs, Christopher Columbus was a visionary. He believed in the dream that he could find the treasures of the Far East by sailing west.

Columbus was told the world was flat and that he and his crew would no doubt sail off the end of the earth. People thought he was crazy for making the attempt. He didn't let obstacles stand in his way or deter him from taking a chance. Despite the naysayers, he championed that the world was round.

He struggled with funding. Undaunted, he persevered and was able to negotiate a deal with King Ferdinand and Queen Isabella to finance his exploration. Recruiting a crew was an uphill battle. Everyone was skeptical. He had to market his ideas and create an environment of confidence and trust.

He is touted for discovering America in 1492. The truth is, there were on-going problems and misdirection. As it turned out, Columbus wasn't the first explorer to arrive here. He didn't actually reach the mainland until his fourth voyage in 1498, proof that being first isn't necessarily as important as being memorable.

Things didn't go as designed. Due to unexpected circumstances Columbus didn't reach the Far East. Still he was a success. Thanks to his exploration to the New World, he linked Europe with the Americas.

Every new business has started with a dream, an inspiration. Like Columbus, despite the obstacles, you have persevered and discovered a way to make *your* business a reality. You are the daredevil, the dreamer, the explorer, the risk taker of the 21st Century.

Do you feel tired and frustrated? Does it feel like most of your time and efforts are spent in a crisis management mode? Instead of increasing your profitability, has your main goal become to stop hemorrhaging money?

When you first started your business, what were you hoping to accomplish? When was the last time you felt inspired; dared to dream? Why should someone buy from you rather than anyone else? What is your product? What service do you offer? Who is your customer? No one knows more about your business than you.

You don't have to be creative to be successful at marketing your business. It simply requires that you know your product and/or services and that you understand your customer's needs.

That may sound obvious; however, many people are so excited about their business that they neglect to consider the various benefits it provides and for whom.

The key is to be specific. What is noteworthy and special about your product or service? Generalities can be made based on industries but just as each person is unique so is your business. It is special, if for no other reason than, because it is a reflection of you and your values and work ethic.

Whether you are creating your business to last a lifetime or to eventually sell it, you need it to grow, to evolve. Marketing and sales should be integrated into the daily activities of your business.

This book is a tool for the fledgling entrepreneur or seasoned entrepreneur desiring to increase sales. You possess the ability to think for yourself and accomplish great things. *Sell More* will help catapult your business in the direction of your goals. It is for underlining, highlighting and more than anything it is for using.

Your answers to the questions peppered throughout these pages will provide insight to possibilities for your company's growth. Take pen in hand and write down the answers to the questions in this *Introduction* and the chapters that follow. They will be a tremendous resource as you create your Marketing and Sales Plan. The specific suggestions and strategies that are included can easily be adapted to fit your unique circumstances and budget.

Applying the ideas in this book will do for your business what slow motion did for Baywatch; they will increase interest in your product or service. Dare to break away from the status quo.

Without making dramatic changes in your day to day operation or spending lots of money, you can make a radical improvement in your company's visibility, sales and profits. The goal of this book is to help you achieve the thriving, profitable business that you envision.

Chapter 1

✦

Sensory Overload, tune into station WIIFM
(What's In It For Me?)

Everyday we are bombarded by over 3500 commercial messages vying for our attention. Like a repetitive sound that you can't shut off, some are irritating and frustrating. Like a car alarm, some have become so common place that they are easily ignored. Like a pesky fly, some are downright annoying and some we tune out completely.

Advertising is everywhere. Consumers are suffering from sensory overload. They have become numb to the many commercial messages on TV and radio. Publications couldn't exist without advertising. Billboards and signs are everywhere we look. Banner ads march across our computer screen. People are dressed as everything from a slice of pizza to a cell phone each pointing the way to the best deal in town. Coupons fill your mailbox. Students are holding placards promoting their club's car wash. Vehicles are wrapped in advertising that until now was only seen on race cars. Buses and trains are covered inside and out with ads. Competition for consumer's attention is relentless.

Professionals and businesses that never would have thought it proper to advertise before are everywhere now. Doctors, lawyers, even the Indian Chief from the Village People, advertise today. Nothing is off limits. Hospitals vie for patients. Pharmaceutical companies promote the latest remedies for anything that ails you and insurance companies are competing for your premium dollars.

No wonder iPods, satellite radios, "on-demand" Podcasts, mp3 players, and TiVo have become so popular. People want to select what they see and hear and when. We register to be on no-call lists; we purchase SPAM filtering software, and use pop-up blockers to deflect unwanted messages and interruptions in our day. Consumers are no longer passive viewers. They want to have control over the flow of information.

Everyone marketing their business is in competition for attention. The key is to create a plan that works for YOU and YOUR business. A small business isn't just a little version of a big corporation. You have unique goals and a very different budget.

Your marketing plan needs to include methods to measure the return on your investments, in other words, sales should result. Brand name recognition is good but sales are better.

How or why will your product or service benefit your customer? This is what you need to convey. Does it taste good? Is the sound fantastic? Does it look great? Maybe it's durable, safe, fun, easy to use, and reliable, saves time, increases production, or costs less. It could be your service, attention to detail, money back guarantee, convenient hours, location, free shipping or cutting edge technology that makes the difference. Whatever constitutes your competitive edge and creates a benefit for consumers is what you want to emphasize.

Remember your message isn't just about you; it is about what you can do or provide for your customer. Spotlight your unique selling feature. People tune into **WIIFM**, the station that focuses on **What's In It For Me**. Information should be relevant, accurate, and brief, to the point and hold interest.

Don't ramble on and on, keep it simple. The message should state what you can provide for your customer and how it will benefit them. Once they know what you do, what you offer, be sure they know where you are and how they can purchase from you.

All too often, people feel the need to take advantage of the many fonts, sound effects and ways to make their marketing materials look, feel, and sound unusual. Be careful. Taking "artistic license" can detract from the person's ability to understand your message.

Avoid outlandish claims. Eliminate deception, no bait and switch, no cheap gimmicks. You don't want a potential customer to feel turned off, resentful, misinformed or even angry. Studies show that a dissatisfied customer will tell ten to twenty people about their experience. Your reputation is everything. Never underestimate the power of word-of-mouth marketing. Good or bad, it can make or break your business.

With so many messages out there, people are becoming desensitized. In order to harvest an enlarged customer base, you need to think beyond the box. Traditional channels are important and should be valued, but if you are getting an "attention busy signal" you need to stretch beyond the expected.

Dare to be different, to be memorable in some way. Every business has the opportunity to be remarkable however very few dedicate the time to execute the possibilities.

Don't rush to make marketing decisions based on deadlines. Thought is required. Make decisions based on where your customer's lifestyle takes them. Where will they be able to view or hear your ads? Where will your promos have visibility?

Thanks to the explosion of digital technology, the methods to spread your message have increased dramatically. There are new distribution channels. Computers, mobile phones, Blackberries, iPods all are vehicles to get your message directly to the consumer. The methods you use will depend on your business objectives, the consumer you want to attract and the image you wish to reflect. Leverage technology.

The web and the Internet offer a world of opportunities to promote your product and services. The Internet represents one of the greatest economic revolutions in history. More and more people are using technology to find the products and services they need. Mark Burnett, television producer and writer has noted that, "The new prime time is 9AM to 5PM because more people have access to a computer then."

Today's digital era has dramatically increased communication opportunities. Thanks to e-commerce, new gateways to permission marketing are now available. Consumers can elect to sign up and register to receive discount coupons, notification of sales, specials and newsletters.

The competition for consumer's attention is enormous. It is harder to get noticed and remembered today. You need to stress how and why your product or service will benefit the consumer. What need does it meet? What solution does it offer? Your message needs to answer the customer's question, "What's in it for me?" Make sure your advertising has relevance, and that you remain tuned into station **WIIFM**.

You need to continuously re-evaluate the methods you are using and your message. Consider integrating your marketing across a broader network of partners. Just as large corporations showcase their brands in movies or invest to have their names on sports arenas and entertainment venues, you need to leverage the tie-in opportunities that are available to you. Consider radio remotes, sponsoring teams and participating in community events.

In order to sell more, you need to make sure you are visible. Customers need to know you exist and what benefits your product or services offer.

Consumers are fidgety and fickle. Their time is overburdened. They are bombarded with information and choices. Differentiate yourself from your competition. Remember if you want your message to convert to sales you need to broadcast it on "*WIIFM*". Give potential customers a reason to say yes, to make a purchase and come back for more.

Chapter 2

◆

"You had me at hello."

You have one chance, only one chance to make a first impression. It has been said that people will make a judgment about someone within the first two minutes. Some estimate that a first impression takes only 30 seconds. Malcom Gladwell the author of *Blink: The Power of Thinking Without Thinking* states that, "Snap judgments are, first of all, enormously quick. They rely on the thinnest slices of experience. They are also unconscious."

It is much easier to impress someone initially than it is to reverse an opinion. Once an impression is made it is difficult to change. Sales are either made or lost based more on perception than price. Real or Memorex perception is reality to your customer.

The way you are viewed from the moment of first contact creates an instant image of your business. It is your "hello." You need to pay attention to every detail; view yourself from your customer's perspective. The way people perceive you and your business, your image, is your "brand." Your "brand" needs to be the cornerstone of all your marketing plans.

You want to create an initial impression that shows that you can provide a valuable product or a needed service. The opportunity to create a positive first impression may begin long before there is any in-person contact. You need to make sure that anything and everything that has your name on it reflects your business in a positive and favorable fashion.

Does your business card introduce you and your business in a clear and easy to read style? Here are some tips and things to keep in mind: Avoid using a Post Office Box address. It creates a "buyers beware" reflex. Your business appears to be temporary or perhaps not real at all. If you are working from your home and can't use your home address, it is worth the investment to rent a mailbox from a UPS Store or other company that can provide a suite or street address for your company.

Is your logo distinctive? Does the name of your company identify your business? If not, add a word or phrase that clarifies what products or services you offer.

All contact information should be in an easy to read font. If you have a website, be sure that the URL, your web address, is included on your business card and all promotional materials.

The way you answer the phone creates the all important introduction to your business. Answer all calls by the 3rd ring. If a customer has to hear incessant ringing they will hang up and call someone else. Be sure to identify your business and yourself. People need to know they have reached the business they were calling; giving your name adds both a personal and professional touch. The tone of your voice should be friendly and professional. It is important to speak clearly and at a moderate speed. Too fast and you may not be understood. Too slowly and you don't exude confidence.

Do you have a separate business phone? If the phone number for your business is your personal cell phone, be sure to create a separate ring tone that alerts you to answer professionally. It doesn't matter if you have a "virtual" business, an office, or work from your home, you want your customer to have confidence that you can provide what they need and that you deliver on your promises. Whether your business is a storefront, a factory, the local Starbucks or located in your garage, your location shouldn't define you.

Voicemail is a great way to capture messages when you are unable to answer. Make sure that your outgoing message is clear. Thank the person for calling and request the information needed to return the call. Be sure to return all calls promptly. It is important not to miss a single call. You may choose to subscribe to an answering or forwarding service through your phone company. Another alternative is to hire someone to schedule appointments and take messages, or enlist a virtual receptionist. Always check out any service or option carefully before signing a contract. Whenever possible sample the service on a trial basis first.

Do you have a storefront location? If so, go outside and enter as your customer would. Is there sufficient parking? Do you have a creative window display? How does your signage look? Is everything clean? Are the product displays organized and easy to access? How does your business smell? All senses are involved in that first impression. What are you and your staff wearing? Do your employees have product knowledge? Are they prepared to offer stellar customer service? Have they been empowered to address any issues that may arise?

Everything from the temperature of the environment to the greeting by your employees will effect the perception your customers have of your business. Does your location reflect the image you want? Do consumers feel welcomed? Is your staff ready to be of assistance? If you give out samples, does your greeter explain what they are sampling and direct the consumer where they can find it? If you have a dressing room, do you offer a place for a spouse or friend to wait in comfort? Is someone available to get a different size or item if it is needed? The customer shouldn't have to get dressed in order to get another item to try on. Paying attention to the smallest details can make the biggest difference.

If you do business on the Internet, it is important that your website is user friendly. Does it load quickly? Is it easy to find data or do your customers get lost trying to access information or placing an order? Can your visitors register to receive additional information and/or savings? Do you respond instantly to e-mails? In a later chapter we will share some tips for maximizing your online presence.

Participating in tradeshows can provide an excellent way to introduce and showcase your product or service. Your booth should mirror your image. Avoid clutter. A well-appointed booth shows that you have pride in your business. Consider the flow of the room when setting up your lay-out. Make sure you will be able to maintain eye contact with your potential customers.

If scheduled appointments are part of the show's agenda, invest in comfortable seating. When a conference table is needed, a round table is better than a square one. A square or oblong table means you each have to take sides. When you are giving out samples, make sure you don't run out and pay special attention to hygiene whenever food is used. If your booth is reflecting a theme, be creative and make it memorable.

Do your ads and promotional materials focus on how your product or service can be of value to potential customers? Think of your message from the customer's perspective. Do they grab potential customer's attention and create a desire to purchase your product or service?

How do you and your staff dress when you are representing your business? Is it an appropriate image? At presentations, are you prepared? Can you clearly articulate the benefits of your product or service? People will evaluate not only the way you look but also your behavior. Are you self assured and confident?

Keep in mind that how you say "good-bye" is a critical ingredient to creating a positive first impression. Your good-bye is as important as your hello. It doesn't matter whether you are doing business at a storefront location, via the phone, or online, it is important to say thank you and invite customers to visit again. You may want to send a "thank you" e-mail or snail mail card, to show appreciation for their business and remind them of the additional products and services you offer. The goal is to encourage customers to return and to recommend your business to everyone they know.

Take time to evaluate what type of first impression your company makes. What is your customer's perception? If necessary you may need to make some changes.

Perception becomes our reality when our brains respond to stimuli. Sometimes our response is accurate and sometimes misinformed. You may know that you offer quality products and services but unless customers perceive that same quality and value you won't have sales.

Taking time to make a positive first impression should be the first ingredient of your marketing plan. Consumers that perceive that your business offers and delivers quality products and services at reasonable prices will buy from you. Once you have a customer, the best way to establish loyalty and earn repeat and referral opportunities is to provide experiences that exceed expectations.

Chapter 3

◆

Market Research: What you really need is membership in "Psychic Friends Network."

The mere mention that it is time to do market research can send echoes of groans through a meeting room. For years market research has been considered a necessary evil, a time consuming activity that produces little in the way of revenue increasing results.

Many businessmen would rather buy a mailing list or randomly follow what everyone else is doing. It is either do that or procrastinate. It can seem overwhelming to research and discover what characteristics define their client base so they can effectively target their marketing dollars.

Many entrepreneurs prefer to try a little bit of everything instead of taking the time to design a specific plan. They think developing a goal oriented strategy means investing hours in research, charts to fill out and worst of all that it will be costly.

The old way of coming up with an idea, doing market testing, and then launching a campaign is too slow for today's fast paced world. On the other hand, becoming a "Lemming" and simply doing what others have done can be both ineffective and expensive.

Conventional market research is being replaced with personal interaction and observation of customer's behaviors. Jean-Pierre Petit, who heads Nike's soccer business in Europe said, "Our designers and product people go to soccer games, or to the in-line skaters at Trocadero to connect with kids. You can learn a lot from watching and talking with them." Today companies are focusing on direct insights instead of relying on statistics or surveys.

Marketing isn't just a task that needs to be done. It is an essential ingredient in the selling and distribution of your product or service. It defines your way of doing business. Its purpose isn't to fool or trick people into purchasing your product or service. Your goal is to educate potential customers that you provide what they need at an affordable price.

Marketing requires an investment of both time and money. Consequently, you need to require a positive return on that investment. Some people believe that "getting your name out there" will inherently result in customers. In truth, it isn't what your name is that matters, it is what it represents. Creating an "I want" desire is more important than an "I've heard of them" result.

Some entrepreneurs knew at the onset who their target consumer was, however as their business evolved they haven't taken time to stop and re-evaluate. Without realizing it their customer base may have shifted or even expanded and now provides an untapped resource.

It's time to review your marketing strategies, your product, and your customer's needs. No one knows more about your business and goals than you do. Maybe it's time to look at things in a fresh perspective and shake them up a little. Be open minded to new possibilities.

Are you focusing your efforts on areas that provide the highest returns? Doing an internal audit will help you discover what works and what doesn't. It will expose areas of opportunities: Pricing? Distributions systems? Customer service? Emerging markets? Non-competing alliances?

Companies spend money gathering information about their customers, demographics and buying trends. Rarely do they investigate the level of satisfaction that exists with their product and services.

How do your customer's measure you? Your product? Service? Price? Performance? Uniqueness? Value? It would be helpful to possess the ability to read minds. Unfortunately, you aren't a member of "Psychic Friends Network." It is best not to assume, instead ask. Even more important, listen to what is said.

The keys to an effective Marketing Plan are to create an environment of comfortable communication and establish goals.

You want to invest your marketing dollars in methods that result in sales. The best resource for marketing ideas is closer than you think. Gathering insights from your employees, vendors, customers, family and friends is more important than the expertise you can get from a high priced Advertising Agency. They know you, your business and your product and can become a tremendous resource.

Your sales staff is the best conduit you have to gather opinions from your customers. What is the point of hiring bright people if you don't listen to them? You need to create an atmosphere that promotes the sharing of insights and ideas. Leverage the creativity within your organization.

Do you encourage your staff to use their initiative and share ideas? Do they feel suggestions are welcome or a waste of their efforts?

Think about the commercials that bombard you every day. Which ads do you remember? What catches your attention? Chances are that the type of things you notice may attract your customer's attention as well.

Gather together your staff, some trusted friends, and family, plus an assortment of regular customers to collaborate and brainstorm. During the session, write down all the ideas as they spill forth.

Don't screen out ideas and only champion the ones that meet your current agenda. Sometimes what lies on the cutting room floor could create a better result. Maybe a new direction is what you need.

By the same token, the majority isn't always right. A consensus without facts can be a dangerous collaboration.

It isn't enough to have creative "out of the box" ideas. They need to be bankable. You need to be an informed sales and marketing decision maker. In addition to collaboration, stay tuned to the latest issues and developments affecting your industry. Keep abreast of buying trends. Be aware of what your competition is doing and on the look-out for potential alliances and partnership opportunities.

A calendar can provide a blueprint for your Marketing Plan. Use a pencil not a pen, things change. Begin by asking, how people go about looking for a company that offers your product or service? What resource do they use?

In the past, every business needed to advertise in the Yellow Pages. Then it was considered crucial that every business have a website. No longer is marketing a "one size fits all" proposition.

Chances are if your toilet is overflowing, you will rush to the Yellow Pages and find the phone number for a plumber who is open and available to come right away. Most trades, restaurants, pizza delivery and professional services still need to be listed in the local Yellow Pages.

Don't invest the money, if it isn't necessary. Reasoning that: "you have to do it because we have always done it," isn't sound. If however, your customers respond that they use the Yellow Pages to locate your type of business or find your product than by all means participate. Review any contracts carefully before signing. When you design your ad make sure your benefit is bold and stands out; "Free Estimates," "Open 24 Hours," "Free Consultations," or maybe you offer a "100% money back guarantee." Mark the due date for the ad's insertion and cost on your calendar.

If you have an online presence, you need to budget the expense for web design, hosting, and data gathering. Content should be updated often to maintain consumer interest. E-mails and inquiries generated to your site must receive an immediate response. Deadlines and expenses involved with your site need to be included in your Marketing Plan, mark them on your calendar.

It is important to gather information about visitors to your website. At the very least you want to know how many clicks a particular page receives. Give site guests the opportunity to register and receive a newsletter or notification of future specials. Not only will this information provide a resource to measure the effectiveness of your website, the data can be used in additional marketing efforts.

In the event you have been in business for a period of time, use your historical sales reports plus the feedback from your collaboration and continue to add strategies to your plan. If you had successful sales or special promotions in the past, add them to your calendar. Note the expenses and the profits.

Is your business seasonal? Does the bulk of your business come at one time of the year or is it basically consistent year round? For example: Someone selling mittens in Michigan may need to make their sales during the colder months. Someone selling cake may have consistent sales all year. You need to take these buying trends into consideration when preparing your Marketing Plan and budget. Refer to Chapter 8: *Sell more; Prescriptions for tired sales and drooping profits;* to find ideas that will expand your client base and generate year round sales.

Holidays create opportunities to spotlight your business. You don't need to wait until December to celebrate Christmas or February for Valentines Day. When customers are melting in the summer heat, have a Christmas in July sale. A direct mail campaign that says, "We love our customers" can be sent out anytime to show appreciation for their business. You want to standout among the marketing clutter, invent your own celebrations. Send customers a "Happy Unbirthday" card with a coupon to redeem for a discount. Use your imagination.

All promotions and advertising should contain a call to action. For example: Visit our site and register for notification of specials. The first 250 people who come by our booth will receive (you fill in the blank). Sign up for our seminar by (insert date) and two can attend for the price of one.

Another way to stimulate action and a response is to sell scarcity. Use phrases like: A limited opportunity, one to a customer, or time is running out.

Maybe your offer is new, "never before available." It may be a better version of a service or product, the "next generation" or the "latest in (blank)." Avoid using "new and improved." Customers may be leery wondering what was wrong with the original that it needed to be improved.

Be ever mindful of what you want your marketing efforts to accomplish. i.e. Increase sales 20% by the end of the year. Maybe it is to sell a surplus item in 30 days. Or, double the number of people who use your service during the next six months. It is important to set specific goals and a timeline.

When you establish a sales or marketing goal, determine the criteria you will use to rate the strategy as successful, adequate or a failure. For example, if you created a postcard and sent it to 1,000 customers during November valid through December 31, you might rate the promotion successful if 30 coupons were redeemed. It might be considered adequate if 15 were used and rated a failure if less than 5 were redeemed.

The expense of production and the mailing costs compared to the return on the investment must be considered. If the mailing was sent to *potential* customers, then your goal criteria would be lower. Obviously, you anticipate that your current customer base would be more likely to respond than someone unfamiliar with your product or service.

When a customer first uses your service or purchases your product, ask them how they heard about you. You want to take note of which marketing efforts are working and which aren't. If someone mentions they were referred by a customer, take the time to follow-up and say thank you for the referral.

Monitor, measure, evaluate and re-evaluate your strategies and procedures. If you used coupons in your advertising, keep count of the number redeemed. Track how often a particular promo code is used when orders are placed? Use historical data to compare the success of sales.

When creating your Marketing Plan, include strategies to stimulate repurchase opportunities and entice "occasional customers" to become "frequent buyers." It is crucial to nurture existing relationships. Ultimately, you will want to integrate customers into your marketing process. Their positive experiences and testimonials will perpetuate repeat and referral business.

You need strategies that fit your unique business. Trying everything without a plan may mean that you devour your budget and fail to reach revenue expectations. Don't groan and put off creating your Marketing Plan. Enlist the input of people whose opinions you respect. Doing your own thing doesn't mean you have to do it alone.

Chapter 4

✦

Re-invent the wheel; dare to be a renegade.

There is an old saying, "If you want milk, you don't sit on a stool in the middle of a field hoping a cow will back up to you." It is equally foolish to sit around doing nothing waiting for customers. You need to be proactive.

You need to maximize your visibility at a minimum expense. To be effective you have to dare to be different and explore new possibilities.

You may offer the same product or service that other businesses sell, but no matter how many competitors you have, you always have the opportunity to stimulate interest and create a desire to give your product or service a try. In this chapter you will learn how to take your initial Marketing Plan and soup it up, make it turbo powered.

Discover strategies to build alliances, innovative twists to conventional marketing concepts, and how emerging markets, trends and diversification can dramatically increase your customer base. In addition, be on the look-out, there are often overlooked opportunities to piggyback promotions and increase sales.

Over the years, business owners have been participating in Chamber Meetings and Lead Clubs. They are a tremendous resource for networking. You refer customers to their company and they in turn refer customers to yours.

To significantly grow, it is necessary to go beyond networking and create opportunities to develop partnerships and cross market. You've heard of the phrase, "Six Degrees of Separation." It's the unproven theory that everyone on the planet can, through a chain of random acquaintances, be connected in some way to actor, Kevin Bacon. Much the same thing can be said of businesses.

There are companies that offer products and services connected and compatible to your business. The key is to unbridle your imagination. Creating strategic alliances with non-competitive businesses is a great way to economically increase your customer base.

Don't hesitate to explore possibilities. Keep in mind that most small businesses are struggling to grow. If you present a win-win concept, they will embrace it.

Here is an example of businesses that can easily create cross marketing opportunities: a bakery, florist, caterer, a formal wear store, musicians, a bridal shop, travel agent, photographer, and limousine company. Each business provides a component to a wedding.

Expanding commonalities from weddings to celebrations increases the number of companies with which you can partner; resorts, entertainment venues, and restaurants provide locations for the celebrations. Party supply houses, event planners, rental companies, stationary supply stores, printers and even cleaning services are additional potential partners. They provide decorations, advice, or a variety of items that can be rented for a celebration instead of purchased. Every element from the invitations, to cleaning up afterwards is an opportunity for cross marketing.

This list of companies is long but with imagination it can easily become longer. Now I can hear you saying, "Nice list, *but* how will these alliances increase my customer base? Sure, we can garner referrals but what else?"

Co-op the expense of newspaper ads or a direct mail campaign. Dividing the expense is an immediate savings. When each company mails to their customer base the circulation increases exponentially. The partnership also provides each business with additional credibility. You are judged by the company you keep. Make sure the associations you make mirror the same image you want to reflect.

Co-oping doesn't always have to involve hard dollars. In exchange for being mentioned, a rental car company may offer a one day free rental to be used as a give-away in your promotion. In exchange for suggesting a customer use a particular attraction, restaurant or entertainment venue you may receive complimentary tickets or a gift certificate that can be used in future promotions or incentive plans.

You can share the expense of a tradeshow. Decorations, items for a gift basket, or a door prize can be supplied by companies that want the exposure but don't plan to attend. You may even split the cost of a booth with a business that also wants to participate, but can't afford it on their own or doesn't have enough personnel to staff it.

If you have a storefront location with windows that need decorating, you have a perfect canvas for cross marketing. Give other companies the opportunity to help you and promote themselves at the same time.

For example: If you are a tax consultant and your location has storefront windows, let a sporting good store and travel agency decorate your window. The headline can advise customers, "Make Your Travel Dreams A Reality. File Early & Get Your Return Quickly."

The Sporting Goods store could supply beach or ski equipment and a Travel Agency some posters. Each would also provide signage spotlighting their location.

Similar window displays would be used at the Sporting Goods store and Travel Agency. They want to encourage customers to use their tax refund to purchase sporting goods and travel from them.

Supply the stores with coupons that can be redeemed for a discount on the cost of tax preparation. They will distribute them to their customers. In turn the Travel Agent and owner of the Sporting Goods Store will provide coupons that you can offer to your clients giving them discounts on purchases made at their locations.

Cross promotions are dependent on creating a win-win situation for the businesses involved while providing a winning opportunity for customers. Major companies have learned the value of blending brands. You can find McDonald Restaurants in Wal-Mart and Home Depots. HR Block offices are located at Sears Department Stores. Blending brands and sharing locations maximizes visibility and access to customers as well as being economically smart.

Restaurants, attractions and a wide variety of service oriented companies have created alliances with concierges at resorts and hotels. The resort wins a reputation for having informed concierges, a benefit that gives the resort a competitive edge. The resort guest wins when they receive informed recommendations. The restaurants, attractions and services win when guests make a purchase.

There are tons of possibilities for partnerships. If you repair pools or service appliances, partner with companies that sell pools or appliances. If you operate a lawn service, then consider working with a real estate agent to create "curb appeal." Is your business environmentally friendly? If so, you could hold an informative workshop at a park instead of a conventional meeting room. If you have a doggie day care, invite a club from a local high school to hold a "dog wash." They get the proceeds and you get the exposure. The key is to be open to ideas.

If you teach financial planning or how to use computer software programs, then you may want to align yourself with a lawyer or CPA. The workshops you offer provide the lawyer or CPA with additional services they can suggest to their clients. It sets them apart from their competition and enhances their image as solution based organizations. You increase your customer base and the client enriches their knowledge.

Share in imaginative promotions. A pie eating contest can be held outside a new funeral home. "Life is short, eat dessert first." Pies can be supplied by a local bakery; you might even have a radio remote with contributions going to Hospice. Okay, okay that may be outlandish and too far outside the box but the idea is to stretch your mind and explore possibilities.

If you have a yoga studio or fitness facility, you can partner with a beauty salon. People enjoy feeling good about themselves both on the inside and out. You can also set up demonstrations at the mall or library. You can participate in a fashion show of exercise apparel or work with a sporting goods store to cross promote selling their equipment while promoting your classes.

Alliances help you to stand out and spread the word of your value and benefit beyond what you can do alone. Forging strategic collaborations can help your company flourish.

In addition to cost savings and the increased exposure you receive by cross marketing, there can be revenue producing opportunities. Pay-per-click advertising is gaining in popularity. Most of the major search engines have advertising programs in place. Your website can provide you the added opportunity to not only promote your company but serve as a vehicle to promote others. You can get paid for this advertising. Check online to see which program is most compatible with your company's image and goals.

Be cautious, adding banners, flash animation, java script, or hard to load graphics may distract from your own message or annoy the visitors to your site. Keep ads unobtrusive. You want to increase the versatility of your Internet marketing while maintaining your commitment to accuracy, integrity and ease of use.

Besides creating alliances and partnerships to cross market, another way to increase your sales potential is to incorporate innovative twists to conventional marketing. The old adage, "if it ain't broke don't fix it" is true; however that doesn't exclude taking advantage of opportunities to enhance or embellish.

Before you invest in newspaper advertising, make sure you are getting "the most bang for your buck." We have stressed that it is important to know your customer and that means knowing their lifestyle. This can help you tweak the traditional content and placement of your ads.

Contact the papers in your area and request their media and ad kits. They provide information that will help you determine where and when to place your ads so you can maximize your exposure. The following are some examples to help jump start your own imagination.

Once a week, most newspapers have a special Food Section filled with grocery store coupons and recipes. If you sell a specialty food item, homemade jelly, cookies or any other delicacy this section will give you the attention you desire. This is also a great place to promote a restaurant. If you're featuring a Friday night fish fry or a holiday buffet, tell the readers about it here when they are thinking about food. They might enjoy an alternative to cooking.

If the most read section of your town's newspaper is the Sports Section, consider placing your ad there. It doesn't matter if your product has anything to do with sports. The goal is to get readership. "Winners use (fill in the blank)." "Score success with (fill in the blank)." Use your imagination.

A florist might advertise on the Engagement & Wedding Announcement page or in the Obituary section. If you offer home repair, interior decorating, catering, pest control, lawn, tree or pool services then you may want to consider the Weekend Section or Real Estate pages.

Placing an ad for massage services, a trip to Las Vegas or even a psychiatrist might find a home in the financial pages. Who hasn't checked their stock at one time or another and thought they needed their head examined, a massage, or that they might as well go to Vegas and risk their money on the roll of the dice?!?

Don't overlook the value of advertising in neighborhood papers. While the Internet seems to be replacing the larger newspapers as a source for news, smaller local newspapers are growing in popularity. If you have a trade or offer a service, we highly recommend that you have at least a small line item ad in your community paper.

Once a week, all the local clubs, meetings and workshops post their schedules in the Community Events section of the paper. Read this page carefully. It can be a wonderful resource. If you can provide products or services to any organization listed, you want to promote yourself here. In addition to placing an ad in this section, use the contact information listed for the clubs and organizations and set up a convenient time to make a presentation. Almost any organization or club is looking for a speaker. Contacting them and doing a presentation can get you recognized as a specialist in your field whether it is financial planning, gardening, travel, scrap booking, or wine tasting. Share how your products and services offer benefits and value. Illustrate how your company can make a difference and you will make the sale.

Advertising in neighborhood papers or in nontraditional sections of major newspapers is also often less expensive. This gives you the opportunity to increase the size of your ad. It might enable you to afford a display ad instead of a simple line ad.

Just as you devote thought and planning into the content of your ad and what page or section to use, it is important to consider your timing. Don't spend your marketing dollars to advertise over a holiday weekend. Of course, there are some exceptions, however, generally readership is down, especially over holidays that are synonymous with traveling.

Repetition is a crucial ingredient to a successful marketing campaign. Placing an ad once isn't enough to be effective. Plan to repeat your ad multiple times. Studies show that an image must be viewed up to nine times before it makes an imprint on the mind. Be consistent with *all* your marketing efforts. You may decide to advertise in the newspaper four weeks in a row and compliment this exposure with your signage and a direct mail campaign. Keep in mind that repeating a bad message over and over doesn't make it good. You need to monitor response and discover what works and what doesn't.

Inviting customers to mention or enter a particular promotional code when they contact you by phone or via your website has proven to be effective. Funneling calls through a specific phone number or extension is another way to track response. Incentify the customer, "Mention this ad and receive (fill in the blank)." There is a simple way to find out how your customers learned about you; politely ask. You want to continue doing what works and eliminate those efforts that aren't cost effective and don't result in trackable sales.

Magnetic signs on the side of cars were a popular trend. Now cars, trucks, vans, and trailers are completely wrapped in advertising. It is a cost effective way to have a rolling billboard. Be sure that your company name and contact information is on the back of your vehicle. At stop signs, red lights and even parking lots this is the area with the most visibility. Vehicle wraps can be fun. They can contain messages, your logo or images that reflect your brand.

This revolution in advertising has resulted in the creation of companies that offer businesses the opportunity to have vehicles in other states carry their message. They become "brand ambassadors." Listings of companies that offer this service can be found online. Be sure to carefully consider all the legalities and opportunities before making a commitment. Car advertising is noticeable. It takes your message where conventional media failed to reach, the residential streets.

What do you do with the mail you receive each day? Do you sort through it and dump the "junk" in the garbage? How do you determine what is "junk." Do you bother to open the envelope first or do you just toss it? Consider these questions before you create your next direct mail piece. Chances are your customer is more like you than you may realize.

What gets your attention? Are you more likely to open something that has first class postage on it? If the envelope is colored, would that catch your eye?

Nonprofit organizations are the number one users of direct mail. It has proven to be their most effective form of fund raising. Businesses can learn from these organizations. They are tuned into **WIIFM** (**W**hat's **I**n **I**t **F**or **M**e). They include address labels, or greeting cards, calendars or wrapping paper with their requests for contributions.

You need to determine what will entice your customers. Mailing conventional flyers or brochures that are likely to end up in the trash before your message is read are unproductive. When your direct mail campaign effectively targets your current and potential customers, it can successfully launch your advertising campaign or promotion.

Postcards are an effective way to get your message noticed. It's true that a picture is worth a thousand words. The front of the postcard can be divided down the middle to show *Before* and *After*. This technique has been used for years to sell diet supplements and fitness programs. It can be equally effective for a variety of other businesses.

One side can show a weedy, overgrown or brown lawn the other, "curb appeal." This example will effectively promote nursery, lawn care products and services.

One half of the card can show a person stressed at their desk, or feature a picture of a frazzled parent holding a baby, food cooking on the stove, and in the background kids wrestling in front of the TV. On the other side can be a tranquil scene, or a picture of them enjoying a relaxing vacation. Maybe instead of a picture there is an Rx symbol for a prescription and text that prescribes how your business provides the remedy for their stress.

If your business is in the world of food, you may want to print a recipe on the front of your postcards. Share a delicious use for your product or spotlight the specialty served at your restaurant or café.

As your business expands and grows, use a postcard to spread the news. It is a great way to educate potential and existing customers of your new services and products. In addition to educating and spreading the word about the benefits of your product or service, you want your postcard to create a call to action. Consider designing your postcard to serve as a coupon. Recipients can use the postcard to qualify for a discount or value added feature.

In today's fast paced world, people still take time to read the comics or take note of a funny caption or saying. We see the proof everyday as jokes are constantly forwarded from one e-mail to another. Use humor to gain attention. A good cartoon or funny caption can attract immediate attention and make the customer more receptive to your message. There are several online companies that provide sources of cartoons. Some companies offer the services of professional cartoonists that will design a cartoon to meet your needs. These sites can assist you in getting licenses to use the cartoon for multiple purposes. The cost is minimal and in many cases they provide what you need within 48 hours.

Instead of sending out the traditional holiday cards in December, send out Thanksgiving cards in November. It is a great opportunity to stand out from the competition. Everyone appreciates being remembered and told, "thank you."

It is now possible to put your logo or message on anything from M & M candies to a jumbo jet. Consider mailing chocolate replicas of your business card to show appreciation for a sale. After an important introduction or appointment, send chocolate in the shape of a barefoot with a note, "Thank you for helping me get my foot in the door." Be innovative and be remembered.

You don't have to deliver pizza to distribute a magnet spotlighting your business. Any business can take advantage of this marketing idea. You can purchase business card size magnets at your local office supply store. One side has an adhesive backing. Attach your card. Include them in your next mailing and/or give them away at the time of purchase. When your information is conveniently located on your customer's refrigerator, it dramatically increases the likelihood that they will turn to your business when they need the type of product or service you offer.

Another item that creates attention is sending a key. The key can unlock a real door or treasure chest that is part of a promotion. This gets the potential customer in your door. Maybe the key symbolizes unlocking how to do something. "Attend our workshop and discover the key to financial security." Or "Unlock the mysteries of Chinese cooking." There are numerous ways to use a key in your marketing; "the key ingredients are (blank)," or "the keys to success are (blank)."

Using questions on the outside of your envelope or as a bold headline is another way to grab attention. You want to peak the consumer's curiosity so they will take the time to read your message. The following are a couple of examples: "Want extra money for holiday shopping?" "Wouldn't you rather have money for new designer pumps rather than spending it all at the gas pump?" "Tired of long lines?" Using one word as a question can introduce the benefits of your product or service, "Thirsty?" "Tired?" "Overweight?" "Frustrated?" Whatever the question, your product or service is the answer.

Consider using a catchy or unexpected quote as a way to entice the consumer to read further. Here are a few examples of quotes that can be used to create attention for a variety of companies.

• "Never purchase beauty products in a hardware store."
Miss Piggy

• "Be careful about reading health books. You may die of a misprint."
Mark Twain

- "Buy land. They ain't making any more of the stuff."
  Will Rogers

- "Be nice to your children, for they will choose your rest home."
  Phyllis Diller

No matter what your product or service, there is a quote that can be used to create interest. Follow with the details of your message. Whatever information is included in your mailing needs to be accurate, brief, to the point and hold interest. If there is a lot of text it won't get read. Consumers are interested in what you provide, how it will benefit them and if it is an affordable value.

Thanks to the Internet it is possible to have a "paperless" direct mail campaign. It can include animation, music and sound effects. Make sure that the content can be loaded fast and easily. If a consumer has to wait, they will move on to another site.

Your site visitors can give you permission and request that you send them information. Provide visitors to your site the opportunity to register to receive discount coupons and alerts to special promotions. Take advantage of this opportunity and send out updates on a regular, consistent basis. Keep your message user friendly. Make it easy for them to pass the word along and share it with friends and colleagues. Include a print option that allows readers to print your coupons without printing the entire page and using all their ink. Utilize technology to your advantage while remaining user friendly. You must always provide your site visitors the opportunity to "opt-out" in the event they no longer wish to be contacted. It is your responsibility to make your communications, interesting and worthwhile. You want visitors to "stick," return often, and share your product and service information with others.

In addition to developing successful alliances and adding innovative twists to conventional marketing, a savvy business owner keeps abreast of trends. In today's competitive climate "slow and steady" isn't likely to win the race. As lifestyles change and new competitors enter the marketplace you need to actively investigate ways to differentiate your business. Allowing your offerings to evolve and meet the changing needs of customers can lead to sustainability and growth.

Become phenomenally good at understanding the various applications and uses for your product, your services and the needs of the consumer. Rejuvenate your identity.

Consider the world and environment we live in today. Are there ways you can attract more customers? No one ever feels they have enough time. Major chain restaurants now offer curbside pick-up. Diners call, fax, or e-mail their selection.

They describe their vehicle. The food is delivered to them curbside without it being necessary for them to leave their car, it's convenient.

Everyone wants convenience. To take advantage of this companies are revamping their packaging. You can purchase vegetables and salad ingredients that have already been cleaned and cut. More and more items come in single serving sizes. Thanks to advances in packaging, you can successfully microwave crisp French fries. They have improved the freshness and convenience of packaged foods. Sherwin Williams has created a twist and pour container for their paint. It has a side handle and drip spout to prevent spilling. They are using television and print media to promote this easier to use paint to their target audience, women.

Is there a way to repackage your product to make it more user friendly? Maybe it isn't packaging that offers you an opportunity to reinvent yourself and grow your business, maybe it is your company name. As concern about weight issues and fried food came to the forefront, Kentucky Fried Chicken became KFC and the International House of Pancakes became IHOP. In an effort to reach a younger client base, the Casual Male Big and Tall stores have become Casual Male XL.

Another way to re-invent your business is to find additional uses for your product and services. Your customers can be a valuable resource in discovering alternative uses. Consider the many uses we now have for Baking Soda and Aspirin. Each started with one use but now promotes a variety of uses; from helping to eliminate unsavory refrigerator smells, and whitening teeth, to preventing heart attacks or stroke. Don't be limited by your original uses and concepts.

Services can also expand their customer base by being open to ideas. Day Care for children has spawned other Day Care industries. There are Senior Day Care and Pet Day Care Centers springing up across the country. Corporate consultants are becoming life coaches. They use their skills and talents to help individuals instead of limiting themselves to corporations. Personal Assistants are now working with groups instead of solely for one client. Some have found their niche running errands for seniors who find it difficult to do it for themselves. Others have found success in taking care of those everyday "have tos" busy families can't find time to do on their own.

Never let competition keep you from exploring your own niche. Curad challenged Band-Aid. They did their homework and learned that children were the prominent bandage users. They found their competitive edge by adding pictures to their bandages. Target specific ages, life stages, economics, and life styles that best suit your product or service and you will discover your competitive edge.

Are there changes you can make, additional uses that you can spotlight that will attract more customers? Does your business provide a service that people don't want to, or can't easily do for themselves?

To move forward and grow, you need to be open and receptive to ideas and opportunities. Collaborate and build strategic alliances. Dare to be different when it comes to conventional advertising. Doing the unexpected contributes to making your company memorable. Let trends lead you but never let them define your business. Your goal is sustainability and growth.

Become phenomenally good at understanding the various applications and uses of your product or service and the needs of the consumer. Be innovative and explore new benefits your products and services can offer. Re-invent the wheel, dare to become a renegade.

Chapter 5

✦

We love the underdog but want to be associated with winners.

From the outside you can't tell if a cake was made with sugar or if salt was accidentally substituted. You don't know until you try it. In today's "need to be cautious world," you might not even give it a taste no matter how delicious it looks if you don't know who made it. If Martha Stewart or Paula Deen made it you might be anxious to sample a succulent bite. If however, you discover Ashton Kutcher of MTV's "Punk'd" made it, you might hesitate.

In an increasingly global economy, reputation has become more important than ever before. Reputation sells. There are lots of different ways to describe your business, your product, your service. It is your job to cultivate a positive image with customers, vendors, staff and community.

Bill Gates can accurately be described as the richest man in America and also as a college dropout. Which do you think inspires the most confidence in the business world?

Don't be bashful. No one has a bigger vested interest in your company's success than you do. You want to merit the trust and confidence of your customers. If you've been favorably reviewed in one of your industry's respected publications, or received an important endorsement, or recognition, spread the word. Let prospects as well as your current customers and clients, know about your accomplishments and successes.

In the words of W.S. Gilbert, (best known for his musical collaborations with Arthur Sullivan); "You must stir it and stump it and blow your own trumpet, or trust me, you haven't a chance." Become a walking, talking billboard for your company. You need to practice and be ready with an answer to the age old question, "What do you do?" Your answer should pique their curiosity to learn more. You want them to follow-up with additional questions.

For example, you might answer, "I increase the value of homes so they can sell for more money." More than likely, there will be a follow-up question, "How?" The answer would depend on your business. There are lots of products and services that help homeowners increase the value of their homes. Maybe you are a landscaper, a realtor, a designer, contractor, or rent furniture to name just a few.

Another answer to the question, "What do you do?" might be, "I take the worry out of what's for dinner." Again there are a variety of businesses that can provide help with this daily decision. Maybe you own a restaurant, cater, deliver pizza, or even cook.

The idea is to think about what your product or service offers. Make your message about your value to the consumer, not about you. I'm sorry to tell you but people are less interested in how you graduated with honors from design school and now have your own architectural company than they are that you, "custom design affordable dream homes." Their number one interest is in your value to them, what's in it for me, **WIIFM.**

On the other hand, if you were selected to design a home for someone well known in your community or you won an award, then you should spotlight this on your website and in your promotional materials. You want to distinguish yourself from your competition.

Consumers are skeptical. You need to create an environment of confidence and trust. It isn't bragging to share information about your success or contributions. It gives you positive visibility and credibility. What is the buzz about your company? Silence may be making you invisible. What is the first thing you want people to think of when they think of your company? Sell the merits of your product or service. Don't assume people know. You need to toot your own horn. Be proud of what you accomplish and encourage third parties to sing your praises.

Know the requirements to submit a press release. The key is to be news worthy and keep it factual, detailed and brief. Be sure to include complete contact information including a name, phone number, your web address, the name of your business or organization and whether the information is for immediate release.

The media is inundated with press releases and promotion requests, they get tons of them. Yours should be interesting and compelling; something their audience will care about. This is your opportunity to capture attention by publishing specific results from using your product or service.

You might piggyback your promotion or announcement with a special editorial issue of your local newspaper, a holiday, or theme. Maybe you want to announce that your location will be a drop off point for Toys for Tots. You might submit a photo of you and your staff dressed to celebrate Elvis' birthday. If you own a restaurant, you can celebrate by serving his favorite grilled peanut butter and banana sandwiches. If you manage a gym, salon, or yoga studio you might submit a photo of teachers relaxing or relieving stress as they take advantage of your, "Back To School Special."

Be creative. You want to continuously build a positive reputation and increase your company's visibility. We love the underdog but want to be associated with winners.

If you have a photo and people are in the picture, be sure to include their names (verify the spelling) and attach a signed release form. You need a separate form for each person. Make sure it includes their complete contact information and signed permission to publish the picture.

A photo with a brief caption is more popular and more often used by the press than a long involved story.

Spotlighting your success also spotlights your customers. Maybe you catered a great party, booked a group trip, created an award winning landscape. Or maybe money was saved as a result of implementing your process, or you eliminated a recurring problem, or contributed to increased productivity. Any of these situations can provide a photo opportunity. These pictures showcase your success and illustrate your value. They also make stars out of your customers and may inspire their loyalty. Everyone clamors for 15 minutes of fame.

If you have a retail location, blow up the photos to poster size and suspend them from the ceiling with fishing line, or showcase them in your windows, or hang them prominently on your wall. Post them on your website. People will want to bring in their family, friends and neighbors to see their pictures on display. They will forward them the link to your site. Each visitor, in person or to your website, is a potential customer.

Request that the newspaper send you a copy of your press release, referred to as a tear sheet. It is your proof that your release was published. If you have a portfolio, media packet or promotional folder, be sure to include copies of the tear sheets. Copies of any press releases should also be included on your website.

Do you have an on-hold message on your phone? If so, make sure it sings your praises and entices the caller to remain on the line. Use it as a vehicle to promote the benefits you offer customers, to create a sense of confidence, or urgency. Here are a couple of examples:

- "This is the last call you have to make. Our recognized craftsmen are here to help you customize the kitchen or bathroom of your dreams."

- "We appreciate your patience. Interest in learning the 5 steps to financial security is enormous. Please continue to hold; tickets are still available."

Sharing your knowledge and experience is an excellent way to distinguish yourself from your competition. It helps to establish that you are the specialist in your field. There are numerous ways for you to share your expertise. You can make presentations for organizations and at club meetings. You can hold seminars or workshops at your location, at a restaurant, hotel meeting room, or you can bring your seminar directly to your client's location.

As an alternative to sharing your information in-person, you can create a brochure of tips, a guide, booklet, or manual. A travel agency might offer, "Things every cruiser should know." A mechanic might create a guide,

"Questions to ask before you say, "Fix it." A cosmetologist might give out tips, "Count down to healthier skin." Use your website to share ideas. Create "Podcasts" to educate the consumer.

Distributing this information is beneficial for your customers and is a selling tool for prospects. Valuable knowledge creates demand. That demand will extend to a desire to purchase your product or service.

Many companies are now offering a sample of their work on a complimentary CD or DVD. It's worth the time and effort to design presentations, and prospecting tools that will demonstrate that you are the specialist. It creates a professional, favorable, lasting impression, worthy of a winner. Perhaps you can produce an instructional CD, or a DVD that demonstrates how to use your product or service. Create promotional and prospecting tools that highlight the benefits and positive results your product or service can provide.

Today businesses line up to have their products endorsed by celebrities. The exposure results in sales. Of course, the ultimate testimonial is to receive an endorsement from Oprah. If she recommends a product or service, it instantly becomes a best seller.

Do you have someone in your area who is well known and respected? If so, you may want to see if they will either do a commercial for your product or service or allow you to publish a testimonial using their name. Showcase any awards you receive. Display any testimonials, letters of commendation, or customers' thank you. Feature quotes from the positive feedback you receive on your site. List any awards or special recognition you have received. Spread the word that your customers' consider your business to be a "winner."

The most effective radio commercials are the ones when the on-air-talent says they use the product or have personally experienced the service. Restaurants have been providing food to stations for years. Listeners that hear the raves as the food is being devoured later visit the restaurant to try it for themselves. The same is said to be true after endorsements have been made for orthopedic services, eye surgery, laser hair removal, resorts, golf courses and spas. You can increase the effectiveness of your promotion if you are endorsed by the talent rather than if you simply invest in spot commercials.

Gift baskets have recently gained prominence as an effective marketing tool. They are given to stars at award shows to gain visibility for their products or service and hopefully even result in testimonials. You can do the same thing. Contact the organizers of local pageants and community theatre groups. You can prepare a give-away for participants or the actors on opening night. It could be a catalyst to stimulate interest in your company.

Word-of-mouth marketing is the most valuable tool in your arsenal. Social networks are influencing buyers more than ever before. People are inundated with choices. They are likely to share the pros and cons of the products and services they try. Don't assume your customers like your product and service. Ask them. Ask for testimonials and referrals. Seek their advice on how to make good better.

Harness the phenomenon of personalization. Thanks to the Internet, spreading the word about a company, good or bad, takes place instantaneously. We suggest you encourage your customers and visitors to your site to share their opinions and comments.

Testimonials supplied by happy customers can have a positive impact, resulting in new customers. People gain confidence knowing someone has gone first and were ultimately happy with their decision.

Unbiased third party endorsements are powerful. It can be especially helpful when trying to get an "in" and win a lucrative corporate account or government contract. As an unknown you may not be able to convince management that your company is best suited to meet their needs. Identifying someone who can lobby on your behalf and present your value may ultimately convince the decision maker that your product or service is the best.

Would your business thrive if you targeted a niche? Become phenomenally good at understanding the various applications and uses of your product or service and the needs of the consumer. This will help you determine which direction to take.

Starbucks turned drinking coffee into a gourmet event. It has become a status symbol to drink their designer coffee. A unique language is uttered by customers after waiting in line to place their order. Starbucks opens new locations daily and are diversifying with an ever-growing product line. They are even producing movies such as, *Akeelah and the Bee*. Starbucks is world renowned as a successful business, a winner.

An often overlooked opportunity to promote your business is in times of disaster or need. Life is plagued with the unexpected. Mother Nature may wreak havoc. Scarcity may arise. It is important to be prepared for "unforecastable demand" for your product or service. Coming to the aid in times of need or emergency isn't only important for your reputation and business; it is a crucial ingredient in your success as a person. The true reality is that business is about people.

Whether your company's focus is Business to Business or Business to Consumer, it is always People to People. The key to attaining the reputation

as a winner is to make each of your customers feel like they are winners for using your product or service.

Chapter 6

♦

Customer Service, it's not brain surgery or rocket science; it's harder.

Customer Service is more than dealing with whining or dissatisfied customers, faulty products, or services that don't fulfill their promise. Today it is important to go beyond providing a product or service to meet a need or want. It is about integrating a positive customer experience into all facets of your day-to-day operation.

Every decision should be aligned with your corporate culture from how you treat your staff, colleagues, vendors and customers; to how you position your company in the community where you live and work. Ken Blanchard, co-author with Spencer Johnson of, *The One Minute Manager* says, "Profit is the applause you get for taking care of your customers and creating a motivating environment for your people." Make the customer's experience your competitive advantage.

Consistently provide the promised service or product. Adhere to contract obligations and delivery dates. There are too many choices available to consumers for you to settle for less than what you can be. Quality and attention to detail should be the hallmark of your business.

Encourage your staff to have fun. Surround yourself with people who share your passion and belief in the value of your product or service. Invest in training them.

Whether your company is a business of one or is made up of a team, it is important that each person understands all the applications and functionalities of your product or service. Different responsibilities require different knowledge but everyone should know and embrace your company's mission and be clear on your policies and procedures. Providing the right people with the right information to use at the right time is the goal.

"What Starbucks does magnificently well is treat employees not as pawns, but as partners," says John Moore, author of *Tribal Knowledge: Business Wisdom Brewed From The Grounds Of Starbucks*. "They spend as much time and as many dollars trying to speak to employees as they do trying to speak to customers."

Give employees a reason to hold your business in high esteem. You don't want an atmosphere where they feel like they are trapped in a mediocre work environment. It is important to create a setting of respect and belonging where contributions are recognized and valued.

Recruit the best available people; talent is a critical resource. Motivate, recognize and reward performance. Make it your job to catch people doing things right. It isn't just your employee's skillset that matters, it's their mindset.

Motivated happy employees create an ambiance that perpetuates loyal, happy customers. It instills a desire in consumers to return and purchase again.

Delivering a positive customer experience involves everybody. Each and every point where a customer comes in contact with your business should be scrutinized to make sure you are maximizing every opportunity to make a favorable impression. That includes the technology you use, the people, and the processes. Pay attention to what happens when people first come through your door, call you on the phone, or enter your site.

Consumers are better informed now than ever before. They have become accustomed to individualized attention and have raised their expectations. You need to paint a compelling picture that creates a yearning to try your product or service. Implement strategies that will boost customer loyalty from the first moment of introduction to your company, to the point of sale, through any applicable service, and maintenance. It is important that you not only provide high-quality product and service, the experience needs to be engaging. Customer satisfaction isn't enough.

Common courtesy is no longer the norm; it is rare. Customers have become accustomed to a lack of service. Helpful staffs are becoming extinct. Late deliveries, poor excuses, cold food, and toilet paper strewn washrooms, are all too commonplace. Consumers witness clerks visiting with each other while ignoring them and making them feel invisible. The personal touch has become the impersonal touch.

Consequently, it doesn't take much effort to make a positive difference. What impression do you want to project? How do you want to be remembered? Does your staff understand your mission? Do they accurately represent your corporate culture? Do they possess product knowledge? Can they communicate the benefits of your product or service? Do they recognize the value?

Investing the time and resources to train your staff can bring numerous benefits. You don't want them to simply tell people that your product or service is great; you want them to be specific about the difference it offers. They need to know about accessories and upgrades that might enhance the customer's experience. Do you offer special payment plans, or packages that include value added features? They need to be able to anticipate questions that might be asked and be prepared with answers. Providing accurate product knowledge, knowing suggestions to offer and when cautions are necessary is a crucial element in the customer experience. Learning the details of what they sell and techniques on how to sell it will give your staff confidence and provide your business with the competitive advantage.

Use praise and rewards, not reprimands to motivate employees. Positive reinforcement can boost morale and performance. It is important to recognize employees who give extra effort. Be specific about why you are giving recognition. Praise can have a hollow ring if it is overdone.

It can be demoralizing to never receive a reward or acknowledgement. On a regular basis, make sure that you communicate to each member of your staff what they are doing right. Help them to have the same success in other areas. Provide any tools or coaching that may be necessary so everyone may excel. Stay focused on the solution and not the excuse. The goodwill and increased productivity your efforts reap will more than offset any time and expense you incur.

Some companies have found success by establishing sales or performance goals. Incentives might include tickets, gift cards, green fees, gift certificates, or money. Be imaginative and customize the reward to the occasion and recipient.

Make sure you are creating a win-win-win situation. You want the company to benefit by increased sales and productivity. Encouraging exemplary performance should benefit your staff with the reward of job satisfaction, as well as a host of possible incentives. The consumer should benefit from a positive overall experience as they purchase the product or service that meets their needs.

Always communicate the details of any specials or promotions that you offer. It creates a sense of trepidation if the sales person says, "Please wait a minute, I'll have to check. I haven't heard about that special." This can be frustrating for both the consumer and your staff. You want to instill confidence, not apprehension.

Take the time to teach customer service techniques. Establish crystal clear guidelines for disgruntled consumers. Depending on the type of business, there may be legislation covering your responsibilities. Keep procedures simple and consistent. It makes learning the policies less daunting. When employees are armed with the knowledge of acceptable practices and policies, you can feel confident in empowering them to use their own judgments to resolve issues.

You need to have policies in place that address the various issues that may arise. Will you offer a refund if a customer simply changes their mind? Will refunds be credits towards future purchases, or will you refund them based on how they paid? If paid by cash will you refund them cash, if they paid by credit card will you refund back to their card? Do they need to show proof of purchase, is a receipt required? Address the possible scenarios that apply to your type of business and be prepared with guidelines.

At one time or another, most businesses have to deal with customer dissatisfaction. No matter how good your products or services are, no matter how good your staff are, no matter how devoted you are to great customer service, it's inevitable that one day a customer will complain about your goods, service or how they were treated. It can be a minor irritation, a misunderstanding, or an issue that requires considerable diplomacy and tact.

Customer loyalty is one of your company's biggest assets. You want to be passionate about earning and keeping it. Some people believe if they don't receive complaints all the customers are happy. Wrong! Studies show that nearly 91% of unhappy customers never complain. They simply go somewhere else the next time. Disgruntled customers not only don't come back, they tell others not to use your business too. You need to consider a complaint as a valuable opportunity; it doesn't necessarily have to have a negative impact. In fact, 7 out of 10 people will do business with you again if you resolve their problem. If you rectify the situation immediately the return rate is upwards of 95%.

There must be easy methods in place to report concerns and process returns. Consumers need to have confidence that their problems will be acknowledged and dealt with quickly and fairly. Whether the complaint seems trivial or the customer is angry, you need to give it prompt attention.

If you have a complaint policy in place, you will be able to resolve most concerns quickly. Listening is imperative. People tell you what they want and need in the way they ask questions or in the statements they make. Keep in mind; people have a low tolerance for repeating themselves. Take notes and restate what you heard back to them to make sure that they know you clearly understand their problem. Your tone should be calm and your attitude helpful and empathetic. The emphasis should be on discovering a viable solution not in assigning blame.

Angry customers are not born; they are created from circumstances when expectations fail to be met. Maybe the expectations were unrealistic in the first place; that needs to be determined. You may need to be clearer in communicating and creating expectations. Never "assume" they should have known. When you are struggling with grumpy, cranky, angry customers you need to remain calm and concentrate on resolving the issue. You want to avoid the tendency to retaliate in kind.

The most important skill required to excel at providing a positive customer experience is the ability to listen. It is more than just hearing someone or reading their e-mail, it is about being able to comprehend what is being said.

Distractions can get in the way. Make sure you focus on what is being said. There is nothing more frustrating than trying to explain yourself and having the person you are addressing continuously interrupting you to take a call or giving their attention elsewhere. Give customers your undivided attention. Make it clear that what they are saying is important.

Avoid using words or phrases that might provoke or exacerbate a situation. Instead of saying, "I don't know," you can say, "That's a good question, let me check for you. Are you able to wait?" Instead of telling the customer what they should have done, soften it by saying, "Here's how we can assist you with that. The next time that occurs here is what you can do." You want to diffuse any possible negative situation and work in terms of fixing the problem.

Use easy to understand terms. Neither speak down to nor use acronyms and terminology that may confuse and hamper understanding. Resolving complaints should never be an "us" versus "them" battle. You must be held accountable to practice what you preach. Be consistent. If the customer's complaining persists and moves to the supervisory or management level, don't sell out your employees by creating a hierarchy that inevitably overturns the original solution.

There will be times when you will have to use your judgment to make an exception to your policy. Be sure that the situation merits the deviation. If you make the exception, be sure that the customer understands that your employee was acting within the company's guidelines. If a problem can't be resolved instantly, explain what you can do and the timeline it will take. Follow-up and fulfill your promise.

Keep a written record of complaints and outcomes. Evaluate them on a regular basis. When there is a common thread, address the issue, implement a remedy and eliminate further complaints. According to Donald Porter, Senior Vice President of British Airways, "Customers don't expect you to be perfect. They do expect you to fix things when they go wrong."

Make sure that all your advertisements, product descriptions, and service claims are truthful and accurate. When your product requires directions, include complete instructions for use or assembly. Speak in terms customers can understand. Include any applicable cautions or warnings. Severe penalties apply for false or misleading information. You want to make sure that everything is accurate so that consumers can make a well informed decision. You want to gain their trust and whenever possible exceed their expectations.

You need to be dependable. Your customers must be able to rely on your ability to respond to their needs and provide a product or service they can trust to measure up to the hype. Don't make promises you can't keep. You want to instill confidence.

If you can't *ALWAYS* provide delivery within 24 hours, don't promise that you will. If you advertise that you have a product on sale, make sure you have sufficient inventory to meet the demand. Offer rain checks when items run out. If you offer a service, make sure you don't over promise the results. For example, a common promise is something like, "Participate in our training program and lose 10 pounds in 10 days." There is no way to guarantee that everyone will lose 10 pounds in 10 days even if they follow the program perfectly. Everyone has a different metabolism, results may vary. Don't mislead, be honest.

If you do make specific claims, be willing to back-up your promise. Domino used to promise their pizza would be delivered in 30 minutes or it would be free. The customer won either way. They would get a hot pizza or a free one. Other companies back their claims with a money back guarantee if their customer isn't completely satisfied.

Make sure your customer's perceptions match the reality of what your company offers. In the book, *"Delivering Knock Your Socks Off Service"* they spotlight a sign found hanging in a telephone center. It read, "You can't promise your customers sunny weather, but you can promise to hold an umbrella over them when it rains." Don't promise what you can't deliver.

If you offer prizes or gifts as part of a promotion, make sure you are prepared to meet obligations. Ensure you have adequate inventory and personnel to meet the anticipated demand.

Offering a guarantee or warranty is a powerful marketing tool. It can set you apart from the competition. For example: "No questions asked 100% satisfaction guaranteed; returnable at any of our locations. Bring it back and we'll pay you back." It states the standards you've set and your policy for resolving problems. It creates a legal obligation.

E-commerce is reinventing the customer experience. In many cases there may never be any in-person contact. You need to include complete company contact information and credentials that verify that you are a legitimate business. It is important that your customers know that they can contact you direct if they need to. Publish your phone number, a toll free number is best. Many people are frustrated and will go elsewhere if e-mail is their only means of communication. Be sure to include a list of your locations. A website can bring customers into your store to make purchases, as well as giving them the option to shop on-line.

The Internet has added a new dimension to the sales process. The goal of any website should be to make prospective customers feel like they are actually experiencing your product in person. The text and pictures on your site should be informative so there is no confusion. Use easy to read print, clearly understood audio, emphasize the benefits of your product or service, the value and quality. Make sure your site is easy to navigate. Provide answers to questions such as: What if I have a problem with the product? Who do I contact with questions or complaints? Be prepared with answers concerning payments, shipping and refunds. If you offer a service, be specific about the results that can be anticipated. Share any guarantee or warranty information.

Ease of use, accuracy and accountability should be your hallmark. Make the process to purchase online painless or you won't get a second opportunity. Don't create on-line forms that might frustrate or intimidate customers. Make security and compliance issues a top priority. Internet shoppers guard their privacy and their time is at a premium.

Communication is crucial. Reply immediately to verify that an order or request has been received. Reconfirm the details, price and shipping details. Send out an update when the product has been shipped. When you are e-mailed a question or concern, acknowledge the question instantly. If you need time to research the answer give a timeline as to when you will be back in touch and follow through. Keep in mind that an auto-response is good but a personalized response through e-mail or phone is better.

Solicit input from customers to improve your site. In fact, you may want to go a step further and allow your customers to become actively involved in your site. Car companies are allowing consumers to design their own cars online. Consider making your site interactive. It is a way for a prospective customer to "try on" the experience of your product or "sample" your service before they buy. Consider using audio or video to engage your customers and differentiate you from your competition. You want to reach the reluctant shopper.

More and more companies are encouraging customers to add their comments and reviews of their product or service to their websites. Opening the door to consumer generated content requires that you are prepared for the unpredictable. Post your guidelines and conditions and be prepared to police the posts. Keep in mind that postings may be fabricated. You don't want to censor content; however, you want to monitor it and make sure there is nothing offensive. As an alternative to comments, you may want to use a question and answer format. Visitors ask you questions and you respond. This will give you an opportunity to become recognized as a specialist in your field.

Being customer focused is an important skill. In addition to the Internet, self-service and automation are taking the person out of the personal touch. Consider ways to enhance your customers' experience. Solicit suggestions from your customers and employees. Make sure that everyone recognizes their contribution is important to the growth of your company.

You want to treat your customers like "High Rollers." If you know your customer by name, use it. Personalize your e-mails. They shared their name when they registered on your site; use it to personalize your correspondence with them.

"Remember that a person's name is to that person the sweetest and most important sound in any language." Dale Carnegie

Emotions and behaviors influence our decisions. The smallest things can make the biggest difference. Are your hours convenient? Do you have current publications in your waiting room? Do you call or e-mail reminders of appointments or updates on shipments? Do you make it easy to reorder? Do you offer prepaid return labels? Do you set appointments and arrive on time? Do you offer free estimates?

In this fast-changing world it is difficult for even the best known and respected companies to maintain continuity and customer loyalty. It's not enough to consistently provide the promised service or product, you need to exceed expectations. Can you do something better? Don't become deaf to what is happening with your business.

Never underestimate the power of saying thank you. Reward frequent shoppers and incentify your customers to return. It typically costs 5 to 10 times more to acquire a new customer than to keep an existing one. Customers who trust that you will deliver a top-notch product or service will refer you to their family and friends. Your goal is to deliver what you promise and strive to consistently create positive experiences that will build strong relationships. Patricia Fripp, renowned sales trainer and author reminds us, "It's not your customers' job to remember you. It's your responsibility to make sure they don't forget you."

Become fanatical about creating a positive customer experience. Personalization is what counts. Be solution oriented when it comes to identifying reasons people aren't using your product or service. Act quickly and responsibly to remove any obstacles.

Deliver on your promises. Be a solution based company. Don't waste time on being a score keeper or blame detective. Merit the trust and confidence of your customers. Develop relationships that turn loyal customers into advocates that will endorse you to others.

Walt Disney said it best, "You do what you do so well that when other people see what it is that you do, they want to see you do it again, and bring others with them to show them what it is you do."

All the marketing and sales techniques in the world won't matter unless you create an inviting and positive customer experience at every point that a consumer comes in contact with your business. In person or online it is up to you to make the difference.

Chapter 7

◆

"What if I make a mistake?"
What if you don't?

We have found that at this point, some people who initially embraced the idea to move forward and *Sell More* stop. The fear of making a mistake becomes a stumbling block on their road to success. We've asked you to re-examine every facet of your business and interactions with your vendors, employees, and customers. We've suggested you seek counsel and advice from everyone. Sorting out how to proceed may seem overwhelming. Babe Ruth once said, "Never let the fear of striking out get in your way."

Everybody makes mistakes. Sometimes the biggest mistake is not taking a chance to explore possibilities. We spend so much time considering the negative "what ifs" that we miss the opportunity for an outcome that may exceed our most hopeful expectations.

Being an entrepreneur in today's business environment has never been more difficult or fraught with more opportunities. Persistence is not enough. You need to be willing to stretch the boundaries of your current comfort zone. It takes inner strength and courage to explore possibilities, to seek opinions from others but make decisions based on your vision of your company and its future.

Jack Canfield is the Founder and CEO of Chicken Soup For The Soul Enterprises, Inc. His *Chicken Soup For The Soul* books are filled with insights into various people's life experiences. He's shown us that some of our most renowned and celebrated individuals have achieved their success because they dared to believe in themselves. Some did it despite naysayers saying they were ill-suited to achieve success in their chosen profession. Some succeeded because they had help and support. The one thing they all have in common is the willingness to take a risk even if they might make mistakes along the way.

Mr. Canfield has been quoted as saying, "As you begin to take action toward the fulfillment of your goals and dreams, you must realize that not every action will be perfect. Not every action will produce the desired result. Not every action will work. Making mistakes, getting it almost right and experimenting to see what happens next are all part of the process of eventually getting it right."

- "Walt Disney was fired by a newspaper editor for a lack of ideas. He also went bankrupt several times before building Disneyland."

- "Babe Ruth considered to be one of the greatest athletes of all time, was famous for setting a homerun record (714) also held the record for strikeouts (1330)."

- "RH Macy failed seven times before his store in New York caught on."

Thomas Edison had a terrific outlook regarding mistakes. "I am not discouraged, because every wrong attempt discarded is another step forward. I never failed once. It just happened to be a 2000 step process."

What others considered his mistakes and failures, he considered to be steps to success. It isn't what others think that will ultimately make the difference. It is what you think and more importantly what you do.

Successful people make mistakes. The reason they are successful is because they avoid repeating mistakes. They do their homework and evaluate where they went wrong. They don't let mistakes, failures and challenges stop them from achieving their goals.

We are hoping that you will dare to risk making a mistake. Don't get us wrong, we don't want you to take reckless chances. We aren't asking you to randomly cut the red or blue wire on a bomb. Boom! One mistake then and it could cost you your life. We are talking about taking a calculated risk.

If you haven't made any mistakes for a while, you may not be giving yourself opportunities to risk, to learn, or to grow. No one enjoys making a mistake however sometimes they can provide a major learning experience.

During the designing of the new Pixar headquarters, CEO Steve Jobs reasoned that one centrally located bathroom would encourage interaction between the 700 employees. Instead of using the one closest to their desk, staff would meet different people as they stood in line enhancing communication. Fortunately for the Pixar staffers the idea was identified as a mistake. Multiple bathrooms for men and women were built in the headquarters.

Admitting you made a mistake can be very difficult. You have to give your ego permission to move on and learn from setbacks.

In 1985, Coca-Cola introduced New Coke. Almost instantly, management was bombarded with complaints. There was a public backlash. The American public protested. They wanted the original formula to return. On July 10, 1985, just a few months after introducing New Coke, Coca-Cola Classic hit the shelves using the old formula.

New Coke may have been one of the biggest marketing flops in corporate history *but* the subsequent reintroduction of Coca-Cola Classic led to a significant gain in sales. The key is to acknowledge when you've made a mistake and move on. View it as an experiment that yielded useful information.

Certainly you don't want to lose money or invest time in an effort that doesn't work. However in some cases, unless you make the attempt you will never know.

Does indecision plague you? Is the fear of making the wrong choice paralyzing you? Are you so busy weighing the pros and cons that you stay where you are, "status quo?"

Do your homework; know what is involved in terms of costs, manpower and time. You want to be informed. You want to take calculated risks.

Ask yourself, "What is the worst that can happen if I implement this strategy or go forward with this promotion?" If you can live with the worst, then proceed and give it a try.

"Fundamentally, everything we do is an experiment," said Douglas Merrill a Google Vice President for Engineering. "The thing with experimentation is that you have to have data and then be brutally honest when you're accessing it."

Take a chance and use the ideas in the next chapter to ignite your imagination. We double dog dare you to take the risks to *Sell More*.

What are you afraid of? Is it that you will make a mistake or that you might succeed beyond your wildest dreams? That may sound foolish but it happens more than you might realize. We find ourselves on the threshold of a positive result and talk ourselves out of the feasibility before we even explore the possibility that our idea might work.

We know you can be successful. Please take a risk. Try on some of the ideas. You might make a mistake or two until you find the ones that fit. You may need to tweak them so they adapt to your unique circumstances. Ultimately you will discover the perfect strategies that will make a big difference and you will *Sell More*.

OUR DEEPEST FEAR ...

(From: A Return To Love: Reflections on the Principles of A Course in Miracles)
Marianne Williamson
Author & Speaker

Our deepest fear is not that we are inadequate. Our deepest fear is that we are powerful beyond measure. It is our light, not our darkness that frightens us most. We ask questions, "Who am I to be brilliant, gorgeous, talented, and famous?" Actually, who are you not to be? You are a child of God. Your playing small does not serve the world. There is nothing enlightened about shrinking so that people won't feel insecure around you. We were born to make manifest the glory of God that is within us. It's not just in some of us; it's in all of us. And when we let our own light shine, we unconsciously give other people permission to do the same. As we are liberated from our own fear, our presence automatically liberates others.

Chapter 8

✦

Sell more; prescriptions for tired sales and drooping profits.

As an entrepreneur, your strategic role is to continually evaluate your programs; eliminating those that aren't effective and establishing new ones. Sometimes despite even the best efforts, sales slump and profits droop. In this chapter you will find a wide variety of ideas designed to inspire you and provide a prescription for "Tired Sales."

Read them over; think about the applications that might work for you. Take decisive action to implement the strategies you choose. Evaluate the response. If the first idea doesn't elicit the projected results and fails to revive your sales, analyze why. It could be that the timing was off, or the idea wasn't effective in your market. Don't move on until you have determined why the idea didn't have the success you anticipated. Maybe a twist on the idea is all that is needed. You want to prioritize new strategies in terms of feasibility, time and projected ROI (return on investment).

Are there ways that you can revamp your "menu" of products or services or the look and feel of your company? You want to create an affordable strategy that doesn't erase the foundation of your "brand." You want to keep a sense of the familiar. A little sprucing or tweaking may be all that is needed to catapult your business to the next level of profitability.

It is our hope that the ideas described on the following pages will inspire product innovation and help you discover marketing opportunities that you may have overlooked or not fully explored. Adapt the ideas to fit your unique business and circumstance. Each idea may spawn several applications. In an effort to make this chapter user friendly, we have divided it into separate areas. Each is filled with ideas and strategies that are designed to help you achieve increased sales and profitability.

What you don't spend adds to your bottom-line.

Evaluating your spending habits can identify ways to ultimately increase your profitability. Here are some questions to help you get started.

Do you buy in bulk, only to find the demand is less than you anticipated? Perhaps buying in a smaller quantity would actually give you better cash flow and be more feasible in the long run. Or maybe the opposite is true and you buy on a "need to have" basis only to discover at the end of the month that you could have achieved a savings had you purchased a larger quantity initially. Carefully consider your buying options.

Have a dialogue with your vendors. There may be viable purchasing options available that will save you money. If you plan ahead, you may qualify for a price break. Perhaps you will be eligible for special payment terms that will help your cash flow. Don't assume you know; take the time to ask.

Are you solely responsible for the costs of your marketing and sales campaigns? It isn't necessary to be responsible for the entire expense. Refer to Chapter 4, *Reinvent the wheel, dare to be a renegade*. In that chapter and throughout this book we have stressed that collaboration can bring benefits. Partner with the local movie theatre; customers show their movie stub and get a discount on your product or service when they make a purchase. As an incentive, consider offering a value added feature. For example, a restaurant might give a free dessert when the customer buys a meal and shows their movie stub. If you own a car wash that offers detailing, partner with a drycleaner. Each can provide their customers with discounts for the other's services. Customers that dry clean their clothes are the perfect target audience to have their cars detailed and vice versa. Building alliances, co-oping and piggybacking your promotions can increase your visibility and stretch your marketing dollars.

It is important to remember that the money you don't spend adds to your bottom line. Before you rent that popcorn popper or pay for supplies needed in your next promotion, consider partnering and giving another company the opportunity to increase their visibility while saving you money. Helping other companies succeed while perpetuating your own success is a win-win way to do business.

When your sales are drooping, it is especially crucial to maximize every penny. Look for opportunities to stretch your existing capital and maximize your profitability by cutting any unnecessary expenses.

Excess Inventory

Do you have items in your product line that are gathering dust instead of finding a home with a customer? Do you promote services that never seem to sell? It may be time to reevaluate their salability.

If the items in question are surplus or discontinued, you may want to consider extending your reach to potential customers and sell them via e-Bay, Liquidation.com or another online store. Dave Ramsey, noted author and talk radio celebrity, says he sells his discontinued products on e-Bay. He referred to it as an electronic flea market. Customers can save money and still be introduced to his philosophy and products. Do you have some items you can sell at a discounted price online through a third party source?

Another way to get rid of excess inventory is to base a promotion around the item or service. The idea is to spark a renewed interest. If you can't sell the item on its own merit, use it to promote your other products and services. "Buy one, get one free." "Fill out our online survey and receive a complimentary nylon duffle bag as a thank you." "Receive a free box of doggie treats with your next visit."

Giving away one item when they purchase one is an incentive to your customer to buy and it gives you the opportunity to clear the item off your shelf in half the time. In the case of the survey, you are rewarding the person for sharing their thoughts. You become better informed. At the same time you are disposing of your surplus item. Make sure the duffle bag is printed with your logo; this will turn the recipient into a walking billboard for your company. If you have boxes of doggie treats taking up much needed space, it is worth your while to give them away with a purchase.

Why isn't the product or service selling? Do your customers know it is available? Is the item or service best suited to a particular demographic? If so, are you promoting it where it will get their attention? Is it competitively priced? Could you repackage it to make it more appealing? For example, if you were to make smaller units would they sell more easily?

It may be time to have a clearance sale and deeply discount the items in question to make room for those products and services that are revenue producing. A clearance sale, should be your last resort. Whenever possible, you want to get maximum value from your inventory.

Never forget that you may be able to use excess items to barter for the supplies you need. Another option is to donate excess inventory. It will make room for profitable items, create goodwill, and provide you with a possible charitable deduction to use on your taxes.

Before you head to the Dumpster, make sure you have exhausted all possibilities to convert excess inventory into revenue. At the very least consider if it is recyclable.

Expand your reach. Maximize your online presence.

Today technology is being recognized as a vital tool in a company's strategy to win new business and expand its reach. Websites have evolved from being the equivalent of corporate brochures to direct sales channels. Content and security is being constantly redesigned, upgraded and tightly managed. You need to make sure your tech systems facilitate new sales and growth. If they don't, it may be time for a needed overhaul.

Obviously, you want to attract visitors to your site but it is the visitors' behavior once they are there that is most important. Go online and navigate through different scenarios. If you have a form for people to register, time yourself as you fill it out. Are you gathering all the pertinent information you need? Is anything extraneous? Does your site feature real time updates, is it people oriented and interactive? If you sell online, make a purchase. Taking the time to visit your site as though you were a customer will help to identify confusing navigation, bottlenecks and abandonment points.

Request that a couple of people whose opinion you value mystery shop your site. Maybe the reason your online sales are drooping is because of technical difficulties and not because of your competition or the value of your product or service. You want to optimize your visitor conversion rate and encourage customers to return and purchase again.

You want to streamline navigation to and from your key pages; content, product and checkout. Eliminate any links that lead visitors away from completing the sale.

Identify which features, pages, links and promotions get the greatest response. You want to focus your efforts on the areas that attract the most attention and generate the most revenue. If you are receiving compensation by advertising other company's products on your site, it will be to your advantage to place those ads on the pages with the most traffic.

Experiment with the content on your site. Simplify navigation. Identify areas for improvement in your web design. Monitor how new campaigns are performing and the products that are being sold. Pinpoint trends and make timely changes as needed to improve traffic to your site and most importantly the conversion rate to sales.

You want to market to repeat buyers. Offer special promotions to entice them to purchase again. If you have data on past customers now is the time to remind them of your product and service. What product or service has created the most interest? Is one demographic of your visitors more interested in a specific product or service than another? Identify the features your customers' value. Use this information to target customers with the specials that will inspire them to purchase.

Enhance your product or service portfolio by adding items or categories that are most popular with your visitors. Scale back or eliminate those that are not interesting to them or not selling. You want to give people what they are searching for, what they want and need.

You can increase sales by making recommendations to customers. When a customer makes a purchase, you should send them an instant acknowledgement and thank you for the purchase. Reconfirm what they have bought and the details concerning delivery. This is a perfect opportunity to make suggestions about additional products or services they might want. It is also a good chance to upsell and remind your customer that for only a few pennies more they could have the deluxe version. It is commonplace today to suggest that for a little more money a customer can increase the value of their purchase. It is the marketing genius behind the concept of "super sizing." Even if a small percentage of your customers take advantage of the upgrade, your income increases. It also gives your customer increased value for their money.

More and more companies are using Podcasting as a means to grow their business. The initial appeal of a Podcast was that it allowed individuals the opportunity to create and to distribute their own "radio shows" for playback on personal computers and mobile devices. Today companies use it to give audio tours of attractions, homes for sale, to distribute public service messages, sell their products and as an educational tool. Consider using Podcasting to share tips about your industry or to educate consumers about your product or service. It can be an excellent way to increase your visibility and become recognized as a specialist. The more confident the consumer is the more likely they will buy from you.

Virtual worlds such as Second Life are gaining popularity. People create a computer generated version of themselves known as "Avatars." You interact with other users called "residents." Communicating with each other is similar to instant messaging. Companies are using virtual cities to learn customer's preferences and forecast trends. Products or concepts can be tried out here prior to being launched. This enables companies to work out any design flaws and costly misjudgments.

A virtual environment also allows businesses with reps scattered throughout the world the ability to come together online and meet. This saves the travel expense and time involved in bringing everyone together in one place. In Second Life, a corporation has the ability to OPEN their meeting so other "residents" can participate and voice their opinions; or they can elect to keep their meeting CLOSED and PRIVATE.

Some companies are creating their own virtual cities and communities. General Mills is one such company. They have created their own community called "Millsberry." It is a virtual town that is targeted at children and the young at heart. It is interactive and includes games and a variety of activities. They know that children influence purchases and eventually will be making their own buying decisions. They are effectively using technology to target their customer base.

Currently, it can be costly and time consuming to build a virtual presence for your company. Like any other online marketing effort, it has to be continuously updated and fit into your budget. You can't just build it and forget about it. However, it is worth your time to monitor Second Life, Millsberry and other virtual worlds. You may wish to create your own "Avatar" and see what is happening in these virtual, often 3-D worlds. It can give you insight into buying trends and help you discover what may be on the consumer's wish list. This knowledge can assist you in designing campaigns that will garner consumer's attention and promote sales.

Catching on even more quickly than virtual communities, are online videos. Today an entertaining video clip can be circulated around the world in a matter of minutes. You might show a video of construction underway to remodel a home. Maybe a clip from a seminar or workshop would inspire interest and registrations. You might use humor and have a video that says, "Don't let this happen to you." Feature a funny video of the consequences of not using your product or service. For example: A beautician may show the unfortunate side effects of someone who dared to give themselves a home permanent; or a video could show someone who accidentally hung a door upside down instead of calling a contractor. It isn't always best to "do it yourself." Use your imagination. Make sure your video is appropriate and never offensive.

Like Podcasting, adding video to your site doesn't have to be difficult or expensive. Speak to your web designer or search online for the company that offers the features best suited to your company's needs. Price doesn't determine which is best; it is usability.

Your homepage is your window to the world. You want to differentiate your company from the competition. Remember that personalization, accuracy, and the ease of use, are essential ingredients in a successful online marketing and sales campaign. Continuously keep your content updated and current. Give visitors a reason to return to see what is new. E-commerce can be a wonderful antidote to drooping sales.

It may be time for a makeover.

The following are some areas that may provide you with opportunities to be innovative and chances to implement cost effective changes that will increase sales.

Sometimes all it takes to revitalize sales is cleaning up your location. It may involve some elbow grease or the time to update your homepage. Would a change in décor make a difference? Perhaps a fresh coat of paint or some new fixtures would give your location a lift. Maybe new graphics, pictures, or a change in layout would give your site a fresh look. How would customers rate the ambiance of your location? Never settle for anything less than clean and welcoming.

Would winning a large contract significantly grow your business? Maybe a "credential make-over" is needed. Acquiring additional certification or designation may qualify your company to bid for potentially lucrative contracts. Keep in mind that regardless of your classification you are always responsible to maintain stellar quality and provide on-time delivery. Otherwise you will lose the contract and damage your corporate reputation.

Maybe a few changes or upgrades in the design or production of your product or service would result in cost savings or increased usability and satisfaction. There has been a fundamental shift in packaging products and even services. Food is packaged in individual portions, sized by calorie count (only 100 calories each), pre-washed, pre-cut and ready to use. The colors, pictures, graphics used to package a wide variety of items are designed to attract the attention of targeted demographics. Cruiselines have added amenities such as surfing pools, bowling alleys and "dine when you want to" options in an effort to broaden their customer base and attract the younger, active cruiser. Vogue magazine now publishes *Teen Vogue* and *Men's Vogue* in an effort to take advantage of the increased interest in fashion and expand its consumer base. Panera Bread Company, Starbucks, and popular bookstores have raised the bar and created atmospheres where their "guests" can linger. These locations have become an alternative to "offices" providing the perfect place for meetings and interviews to take place. Creating a comfortable atmosphere results in customers staying longer and studies show customers purchase more. CPAs are now packaging their accounting and tax services as part of a business solution package. A redesign is risky but may pay off in a dramatic increase in revenue.

Even McDonalds is revamping its restaurants. They are no longer considering their customers to be just a number to add to their billboard. Proof that even the most enduring icons recognize that in order to achieve sustainability and growth it is important to stay tuned to the desires of your customers. You must be willing to adapt and make changes. They are adding snack foods and smoothies to meet the demand for between meal refueling and late night munchies. They are redesigning the dining area to include sections for lingering. Their restaurants will even feature wi-fi availability. Change can be good. It is also important to keep a sense of the familiar.

If you have a restaurant, café or bar, consider offering entertainment; it might attract more customers and tempt your regulars to return more often. It isn't necessary to feature it everyday. It can be occasional or on selected days of the week. Use your imagination; it can be music, poetry readings, karaoke, comedians or someone who makes balloon characters. An "Open Mike Night" might provide the perfect enticement to customers. Make sure the entertainment you choose reflects positively on your business.

No matter what your product or service, theme and special event celebrations can be a fun way to attract new customers. You can celebrate holidays, grand openings, anniversaries, and even make up your own special events. For example on Friday the 13th you can have a "It's your lucky day celebration." Give out coupons for a 13% discount redeemable when a purchase is made that day. Sporting events and local festivals can inspire opportunities to piggyback with a celebration or theme a companion promotion.

Advertise and promote your entertainment and special themed events. Consider inviting someone from your local paper to come and cover the event. Generate interest by inviting a prominent radio celebrity to broadcast their show from your location. Take pictures of the fun and post them on your site and display them at your location. Create a buzz that will keep your satisfied customers eager to return and make others anxious to visit and join in the fun.

Do you have background music playing at your location? If so, avoid using the radio. An unexpected commercial may feature your competition and entice your customers to try them the next time instead of returning to purchase from you again. Music should compliment your environment. If you have incorporated music on your site, be sure to have an easy way to turn it off or by-pass an introduction. The volume should be subtle and not intrusive. It should enhance the consumer's experience.

If you have a retail operation, is it easy for customers to find items? Do you have items that go together placed near each other? Are there ways you can regroup your stock that will increase the items purchased? This is a terrific way to increase sales. For example if you sell tools, do you have hammers near the nails, saws near the wood, paint near the rollers and paint brushes? Groupings have proven to be a very successful method to maximize sales. A business that sells apparel may group items by type, season, size, sex, or categories such as casual or formal.

The benefits of "grouping" aren't limited to retail. Consultants group the various services they offer by category, type of business or levels (introductory, beginning, intermediate or advanced). A customer who may have originally paid for advice about one project or a solution to one problem is now aware that your company can provide additional options and resources.

Categorizing and grouping items together has also proven to be a very successful method when selling online. Items are grouped by uses, occasions, seasons, gender, sizes, descriptive terms such as destinations when selling travel, or traditional, modern or antique for example if selling décor. The categories for grouping your products or service are only limited by your imagination. For example, if you are selling spicy food items you might group them together by degree of heat; mild, medium, spicy, fiery, or explosive proceed with caution. Groupings stimulate the consumer's imagination. It reminds them of other items that are available that may have slipped their minds. It saves the consumer shopping time and can increase your sales and profitability.

When you are setting up your "groupings," don't neglect that all important Point of Purchase area (POP). The check-out area of your store or site should contain items that will trigger the desire to make one more purchase. Do you have a product or service you can showcase at the point of sale that will inspire impulse purchases?

Another way to increase sales is to group your staff by their roles, experience and/or responsibilities. Travel companies may offer "specialists" in different destinations. One agent may specialize in cruising; another agent might specialize in affordable family vacations. Beauty shops may spotlight one person as the best colorist; another may specialize in cutting hair, while another may be great at styles for weddings and formal occasions. Best Buy offers the "Geek Squad" to help their customers with questions about their PCs. Apple has their "Genius Bar." Home Depot promotes the fact that their staff, in the orange aprons, is ready and able to answer your home improvement questions. Even if you are a business of one, you play various roles. One day you are the CEO, next you might be the Creative Director, or Senior Technician. Be prepared to showcase your specific skillset when the appropriate occasion arises. Everyone is looking for the best value for their money. Establishing that you have qualified specialists available to help them with their questions gives you a competitive edge. This is a good way to increase consumer confidence and set you apart from your competition.

Is a positive customer experience the goal of your staff? Is customer assistance readily available and easily accessible in person, by phone and/or online, via your website or e-mail? In an effort to maintain accuracy and avoid confusion, do you always state the day of the week and the date when setting appointments, travel departures and delivery dates? Creating a reliable, positive customer experience and being available when questions or concerns arise is an indispensable ingredient in any highly successful business. Do your customer service skills need a makeover?

In today's hectic world of "never enough time" convenience is of paramount importance. Your competition isn't just the other companies that offer the same or similar products or services. You are competing for the consumer's limited discretionary income and time.

People are busy. They need you to be available when they are. It is no longer good enough to adhere to an "open 9 to 5" schedule. This is the age of dual-income families. Everyone is employed, working to make ends meet. Do you offer the option for customers to set-up appointments? Can customers make purchases in the evening, on the weekend, or 24/7 via your site? When doing a makeover, consider carefully if your hours are convenient. Is it easy for customers to purchase your products or service?

If more people decide to purchase their travel on Sunday, after reading the travel section of their paper, maybe you should consider Sunday hours even if all the other agencies choose to be closed. It could give you a distinct advantage. By the same token don't feel handcuffed to stay open when there is no business. If you run a restaurant and the bulk of your business is at breakfast and lunch maybe being open for dinner isn't cost effective. Evaluate your customer's buying behaviors. Set your hours so you are available to maximize sales opportunities.

If appropriate to your business, do you have sufficient parking available? Do you offer special parking for expectant mothers, valet parking, curbside pick-up, or a drive-thru? If you are located on a busy waterway, maybe you need to build a dock. It is all about making your business easily accessible.

Consider negotiating with another business to share space. We've all seen the various businesses that now are located within Wal-Mart. They offer everything from vision services, McDonalds, to photographers. Customers enjoy the convenience of having a variety of businesses located in one place. Maybe there is an opportunity for you to increase your visibility and sales by locating your business within another business or even in their parking lot. Car wash and detailing shops have taken up residence in mall parking lots. The customer shops while their car gets cleaned. Laundromats are creating a welcoming environment for busy people with dirty clothes by incorporating coffee shops. Your goal is to save the customer time and create a positive experience.

Is your business portable? Can you bring it to potential customers? Sometimes the best way to makeover your business and revive slumping sales is to expand your reach. Go to potential customers. Call Centers are situated throughout the United States. Most offer businesses the opportunity to set-up a table in the break room and sell their wares. Some even allow businesses to sell their employees box lunches or do chair massages. Check your local business directory and see what similar opportunities are available for you.

Can you outfit a van to bring your business to customers? You might bring your skills as a beautician to a senior care facility. If they can't come to you, you can go to them. You might offer to go to schools to do massage or yoga to relax overworked teachers. If your business is pet care, you can outfit your van so you can go to homes to shampoo and groom pets. Increase your convenience and increase your sales.

Follow the lead set by Tupperware and offer home parties. People enjoy the social aspects of being with friends. Give the host an incentive to have the gathering at their home. This is a great way to make shopping convenient for your customer, informative and fun. Consider if your product or service could be sold in such a setting. Home parties can increase sales of services as well as specific products. You could speak to a gathering about financial planning, offer healthcare tips, or hold a cooking or craft class. When sales are in a slump it's time to try new things.

Free demonstrations or estimates are another way to show customers how valuable your product or service can be. You want consumers to feel confident so they can give themselves permission to say yes and make a purchase. Demonstrations can be given almost anywhere. High traffic areas such as tradeshows, festivals, home parties and such are ideal. Any demonstration needs to be accompanied by the ability for consumers to make an immediate purchase.

When you evaluate your business to decide if a makeover is in order, consider what impression you want to make. If a customer were to write your company's epitaph what would you want them to say? How do you want to be remembered?

The nose knows.

You want your location or site to be visually pleasing, delicious if food is involved, easy on the ears and smell good. Don't underestimate the power of scent marketing. The nose knows. Aromas can attract or repel customers. Real Estate Agents have long known the value of scent. They have cookies or bread baking in the homes they are showing. The "fresh from the oven" smell creates a "Home Sweet Home" atmosphere. It not only smells good, it also camouflages any odors present from the previous owners or construction. The Omni Hotels use a mixture of green tea and lemongrass to perfume their hotels with a welcoming scent.

You need to be careful that the aroma you choose isn't overpowering and has universal appeal. Incense or strong scents may appeal to you but have a negative effect on your customers. Subtle is best. Thankfully, aroma therapy is currently popular; even the novice can readily find information delineating which scents evoke which emotion.

It may sound funny to ask, but have you smelled your business lately? Even if customers never visit your location, you want to make sure your work environment is free of distracting odors. Perhaps your nose has become accustomed to the smells. It might be the perfect time to invite someone to come and do a sniff test.

Just as bright colors energize, so does the aroma of citrus or rosemary. On the other hand, the smell of lavender or cucumber eliminates feelings of stress and creates a sense of calm in the same way a room painted in cool colors calms the spirit.

If you have a dental practice or offer spa services, you might want to light some candles or spray an aerosol that contains tea tree oil. It is said to ground your thoughts. If you work in a company that is an idea factory, maybe you are a consultant in product development or marketing, the scent of cinnamon or mint might help to spark your creativity.

Some smells have a magnetic quality. Popcorn is a perfect example. The smell of fresh popped corn can draw people from far away to come and investigate its source. Consider filling sand pails with popcorn. Wrap cellophane around the bucket and tie it with ribbon. Attach a brochure or postcard spotlighting your product or service and deliver them to the receptionist at various offices in your area. It is a great attention getter and the news of your company will spread as workers arrive at the desk drawn by the aroma. You can also use this idea as a thank you when you are delivering tickets or information to a corporate account.

Your "thank you" will be appreciated by your customer and word will circulate about your service. When you differentiate yourself in a positive fashion from your competition, you earn loyalty and win new clients.

It is also possible to rent popcorn carts that remind people of years gone by. If you are participating in a sidewalk sale, craft fair, tradeshow, or open air market, this is a great way to entice people to linger and learn about your product or service. Please be careful when popping the corn. Just as the smell of fresh popped corn can draw people in, burnt popcorn can send people running in the opposite direction.

Magazines have been selling perfume by placing samples tucked away between its pages. If you garden or bake, you might consider adding a scratch and sniff feature to your promotional materials or postcard. An online search of "scratch and sniff" will give you a listing of companies that offer a wide variety of scratch and sniff options. Some will even customize and replicate a sample of the scent of your product. It is a fun attention getter that can set you apart from the rest.

If you are working from home, you may want to light a candle to inspire you or keep you calm. Eucalyptus clears the head and invigorates the mind. Pine is believed to stimulate creativity. Thyme is thought to strengthen your immune system. Chamomile is said to bring relaxation. Vanilla is considered an aphrodisiac. A bouquet of flowers on a nearby table can be the perfect way to add a pleasant fragrance to your work area.

Use the power of smell to create an atmosphere that maximizes productivity and creativity. Explore the possibilities of using scent to attract clients. You want to entice them to give your product or service a try.

Time is running out, "I must have it."

Several companies have been very profitable targeting the desire within all of us that says, "I must have it." Sometimes that means only the best will suffice. Sometimes that means they were lucky and reacted quickly enough to get something that others wanted before it ran out or was gone. Sometimes it means they qualified for a benefit when others didn't.

Starbucks elevated drinking coffee into a status symbol. You have to be willing to stand-in-line and know the language to order your special, "tall low-fat decaf cappuccino." Walking around proudly with your cup stamped with the Starbuck's logo, you are a member of the coffee drinking elite. You are enjoying a delicious cup of coffee and you feel special. Ideally, you want your business to generate a desire in customers to make a purchase. You want them to feel smart and special for choosing to purchase your product or service.

McDonald's and other fast food companies have learned the power of creating a heightened desire for their product by offering specialty items for a limited time once or twice a year. What man hasn't detoured through the nearest McDonalds drive-thru when he heard the McRib was back?

Disney is another company that uses limited availability to generate sales. They play on our desire to reminisce and share stories from our childhood with our children by re-introducing movies we loved. DVDs of favorite classics, such as "Lady and the Tramp" or "Peter Pan," are only available for sale for a limited time. Consumers need to act fast not knowing when they may be available again.

Sometimes less can be more. Instead of continuously trying to appeal to everyone everyday, consider offering a weekly special targeted at a specific customer base. If Tuesdays are notoriously slow, offer a special that will attract attention. Create seasonal sales or celebrations that your customers will look forward to. Make your specials unique to your business; don't use the same timing as everyone else.

Special pricing is offered by many companies to attract seniors and/or children. Some businesses have one day a week set aside when seniors receive a special discount. Special "Kid's Meals" and "Children under age 12 stay free or eat free" promotions are designed to attract families and show appreciation for their business. Mechanics set aside one day a week as ladies' day. Offering a discount on an oil change attracts a new demographic to their location.

Knowing your target market and their values will help you determine if there are opportunities for you to increase your sales and profitability by creating a limited time special, exclusive offer, or attract customers with a trend setting product or service. Can you offer a "special edition" of your product or service? Is there something inherently special about your product or service that you can spotlight? Does someone with celebrity status use your product or service that would be willing to give you a recommendation?

When the time and place for playoffs, popular concerts, or appearances by noted speakers is announced, tickets are sold out quickly. Everyone understands that there is only limited availability. There is a sense of urgency and excitement associated with obtaining these tickets. Fans want to be one of the "special" people who get to enjoy the experience in person and not be relegated to the television. That sense of "I want" or "I need" is what you want to create with your product or service.

Offer some items or services that are deluxe, that are premium quality and dare to price them higher. Customers decide to purchase based on value, not exclusively because of price. Just as numbered prints often go up in value, creating a limited number of specialty items may increase the demand and perceived value of your product or service. The key is to match your special to the interest of potential customers.

For example: If you have a base of NASCAR fans as customers, you might want to offer a Daytona 500 special. This idea can be translated to fit a variety of businesses. It can range from simple black and white packaging of your item to limiting participation at your next leadership training class to the first 500 who register. You could offer special food items with names based on racing terminology. A word of caution; NASCAR, Disney and major league sports all have tight licensing agreements. You need to make certain any promotions you create fall within their guidelines and have received the necessary approval or that they are totally generic in nature.

Every business, no matter what the product, offers something that is exclusively theirs. It may be your ingredients, your level of expertise, your free estimates, or 100% money back guarantee. Some businesses find greater success in defying mass consumerism and offering their product or service to an elite targeted group or solely via their website or exclusively through a third party distributor or retailer. Some companies have dared to position themselves by selling only one item. They have become known for exclusively selling cupcakes, or catering weddings or working with corporations that have at least 100 employees. Transforming your business and featuring one item or service or limiting distribution channels can be risky. It might increase your sales opportunities or it may be limiting and not beneficial. Carefully analyze the pros and cons.

We encourage you to focus attention on your specialty; advertise and promote it. What does your company offer that you can position and sell to customers in such a way that they feel "I must have it?" How can you create a sense of urgency so consumers will rush to take advantage of your product or service before you run out? You want to make your brand synonymous with being the best. Create a sense of "must have" in your customers and you will cure your drooping profits.

Create a need. Supply a solution.

Investigate possibilities to increase your sales and income by offering new products or services. Consider expanding beyond the scope of your original business plan. Sometimes diversification can boost sales of your initial product or service.

Andre and Edouard Michelin were considered crazy when they decided to publish guidebooks for tourists. After all, what did people in the rubber business know about publishing? They printed 35,000 copies of the original edition and gave them away free. The guides included information about hotels, restaurants, and roadside attractions. It even included driving tips and maps.

As it turned out, their diversification was genius. Cars were rare in 1900. The Michelin Guidebook inspired people to travel. It created an increased demand for automobiles. Cars need tires and that is exactly what Michelin rubber was able to provide. The guidebooks not only helped to increase the need for cars, tires needed to be replaced more frequently because people were traveling further, anxious to explore the places mentioned in the guides.

Are there goods or services that you can offer that will compliment your current product line? Where would digital cameras be without the PC? Movie theatres make more money selling concessions than showing first run movies. Interior decorators are now staging homes to help realtors and homeowners sell their homes faster and for the highest price. It gives the decorator added income and exposure. This often results in the homebuyer or open house visitors hiring them to decorate their home.

Printers have recognized the increase in homebased businesses. They are capitalizing on this trend by selling stationary packets complete with business cards, letterhead and envelopes. This is a value for the entrepreneur. Many times this results in the printer garnering additional sales printing brochures and collateral materials.

Identify a trend and find a way to create a sales opportunity from it. Jeff Grady is the President of Digital Lifestyle Outfitters. In 2001, after spending over $300 for a new gadget called an iPod, he decided he needed a case to protect it. None was available. Consequently, he designed and made one himself. He called a buyer at Apple Accessories about his idea. Almost immediately they placed an order. This launched his company. According to an article in Inc. Magazine, September 2006 written by Patrick J. Sauer, "Digital Lifestyle Outfitters sold $84 million dollars worth of cases, boom boxes and other iPod accessories in 2005."

Is there an innovative idea percolating in your mind that can provide a much needed solution, fill a void, or create a "got to have it" need? Innovating, diversifying or expanding your product line can pay off by increasing your revenue streams. A word of caution, you don't want to diversify so much that your original brand and reputation for quality get diluted.

Be vigilant. Focus on earning a positive return on your investment. Study the dynamics of your business. There may be opportunities to be creative and add to your core product line that will give you a competitive advantage and perk up tired sales and drooping profits.

Niche Marketing

Chasing every customer can be a waste of time and resources. You need to identify who can benefit from your products or services. You need to scrutinize your customer base and determine if different demographics have different uses for your product or services. Is there a way to better target your marketing and expand your current customer base? Every company would benefit from being studious and learning their customer's buying behaviors and then creating a niche marketing plan that will attract attention.

It is important to do your homework. No matter who your customer is the better you know them the easier it will be for you to sell them your product and service. Successful selling is, synonymous with building win-win relationships.

If your niche is other businesses and corporations, invest the time to learn who the decision maker is. You want to know their first and last name (confirm the spelling) and their correct title and responsibilities. You don't want to go on a scavenger hunt when calling a potential client. You want to know who you need to address.

Learning a little about the company will give you an advantage when making your pitch. Being informed enables you to give specific examples of how your product or service will benefit them. Search the Internet and read the company's current press releases. There may be a little known fact mentioned. It can give you an opportunity to show that you took the time to do your research when you congratulate them on a special achievement or mention something specifically related to their operation. Thanks to the Internet, information can be accessed quickly. Even so, very few people take the time to do their homework and warm up their cold calls.

Knowledge is a powerful tool. It will instantly set you apart from your competition and increase the odds that you will make the sale.

Most companies treat their customers all the same. They fail to differentiate. We could fill pages upon pages with different ways you can distinguish your clients. It can be as simple as male, female, or seniors, families, children, or geographically, or by common interests, cultural, or ethnic distinction. There are limitless possibilities. Just like corporations, consumers are selective about what they permit into their sphere of influence. Customers build a mental fortress against being bombarded by incessant advertising. One way to avoid being filtered out is to target your Marketing. Cater to unique demographic needs.

Revealing who your customer is will not only determine the most effective ways to present your products or services, it effects the way you setup your distribution system. You need to have the right inventory on hand to meet the demand. Your services need to be appealing. A simple miscalculation of what is expected can lead to a loss of sales, alienation of customers, and unproductive inventory definitely resulting in drooping profits.

Keep in mind that the manner in which you speak contributes to sales or customers leaving without buying. Accents and colloquial slang may be charming in one's personal conversations but can be difficult to understand by your customers. Before you ask someone to represent your company and speak directly with customers, make sure they are trained and can clearly articulate the uses and benefits of your product or service. Also emphasize the importance of body language. Your staff needs to feel confident and comfortable answering any questions potential customers may have.

America is a melting pot of people with various ethnic backgrounds. If your target audience speaks Spanish, make sure someone on your staff speaks Spanish. Just as it can be frustrating for a customer if no one speaks their language, it is becoming equally frustrating to discover that no one at the check-out speaks English. It is important that anyone who is responsible for direct consumer contact be fluent in the required language and have strong communication skills.

As a general rule you want to avoid using industry jargon. Ask someone who knows nothing about your product or service to listen to your sales pitch. Request that they review your promotional materials and the text on your site. You may inadvertently use terms that are commonplace to you but confuse your client. If a customer feels confused or frustrated because they don't understand something, they may go elsewhere. They may feel more comfortable talking to someone else rather than admitting to you that they don't understand.

There are exceptions to every rule and there are occasions when your targeted customer base will need to know that you are familiar with the terminology of your niche. If you sell golf equipment, customers need to know that you are familiar with the intricacies of the game. They need to know that you know the term "links" and don't think it refers to sausages. Although using technical jargon can turn away business, there are specific cases when using industry terminology will increase the customer's confidence. The key is to present the message about your business in a manner which is easy to understand. It should speak to the needs and interests of your targeted audience.

Stereotypes rarely apply anymore. No longer can families be defined as a man and a woman (husband and wife), with 2.2 children and a dog. Single parents are commonplace. Grandparents are raising their grandchildren. Same sex life partners are becoming parents. There is no longer one definition of family.

As lifestyles change, companies need to look for new opportunities to grow their business. It is becoming rarer for mothers to be able to stay at home with their children. The high cost of living is making it necessary for both parents to work. Out of economic necessity, children are starting day care while they are still infants. Does your product or service offer a benefit to these newly defined families and their lifestyles?

Not all areas of the country have the same needs, culture and values. There are regional differences just as there are differences in sex, age, and language. You can profit by understanding who buys your product or services and the way they are used. This will enable you to target and cater to your customers' demographic.

Cancer survivor and seven time Tour de France winner, Lance Armstrong said, "It's not about the bike—it is about the person riding it. It's not about your product—it is about the people who use it, build it, sell it and manage it. Your challenge is to find out the specifics about what people who buy and use your products and services REALLY want so you can enhance the total experience they have in dealing with your organization."

Harness the power of personalization. Don't try to be everything to everybody. Identify your "niches," use creativity and maximize your sales opportunities to these targeted groups.

If families visit your business or site make sure the environment is child friendly. Is there an area set aside where children can play safely or watch a video while their parents shop or get their car serviced? Are there supervised activities offered to occupy the children while the parents enjoy your resort, exercise at your fitness center, or see a movie at your multiplex? Offering supervised activities or babysitting can become a revenue generating service.

Children were once considered a distraction when they accompanied their parents to a place of business, a gym or restaurant. Today it is recognized that appealing to children can extend the purchasing cycle. Attracting children into your market segment will help you maintain your market strength for years. Not only do they influence their parents to purchase today but when they hit their teen years they often have tremendous buying power especially for high-demand products like gaming technologies, grooming products, fashion and music.

If you have a website or business that targets teens you want to make sure to convey it's a "not where their mom or dad or little sister shops" environment. Your business needs to be interactive. Teens like to "try it out" first before they buy. Showing videos, streaming popular music and offering online games will engage teens and keep them interested. Providing them opportunities to share their thoughts and opinions on message boards or blogs is important. A great way to keep abreast of what is current and stay in touch with new trends is to read what your customer reads. Sometimes that means you need to read *Tiger Beat* or *Seventeen* magazines. Targeting the youth of today can reap benefits and result in customers for years to come.

The current slowdown in home sales has been accompanied by a surge in people remodeling their residences. This provides an opportunity for various companies to expand their customer base by tapping into this trend. Outdoor space is now living space, no longer just a yard with a swing or maybe a garden. Consumers are investing in decks, gazebos, and outdoor kitchens. Designers are creating all-weather materials and products. The demand for help from architects, contractors, electricians, carpenters, plumbers, gardeners, interior designers and remodeling services and supplies is growing. Does this trend to remodel or restore rather than sell, create a growth opportunity, a niche, for your business?

On the other hand, the slowdown in home sales may make your skills and ability to sell properties more valuable than ever. Do you offer services to stage a home? Can you assist with curb appeal? Are your painting and handy man skills needed to fix up a "fixer upper" so it can be sold for top dollar?

A downturn in sales in one area can create sales opportunities in another. You need to stand back and view the whole situation and then develop a strategy that allows you to position your products and services so they can fill a need for the customer and result in revenue for your business.

84 million people were born between 1946 and 1964. They are defined as the "Baby Boomer" generation. This demographic has a powerful influence on our economy today. People are living longer and are more active. They are using the "new math" to recalculate their age. Most feel young despite what the calendar says. Smart companies are targeting this demographic. Baby boomers feel younger and want to look younger. They are perfect candidates for health, beauty, and fitness products. They want to make their outside match the way they feel inside. Meals for two are designed for "empty nesters." Travel agencies target them for longer vacations. Many of today's seniors have both the time and

funds to enjoy extended travel opportunities. These 84 million people provide millions of sales opportunities.

Many baby boomers plan to work past the typical retirement age of 65. In fact, some of you using this book may be perfect examples of this. Age is just a number. Unlike their parents, many baby boomers see no reason to retire. Unfortunately, layoffs and other economic challenges have caused some to search for new employment or change careers entirely. Do you run a staffing company, specialize in resume writing or offer training that can prepare this seasoned workforce for new opportunities? If so, this reservoir of potential customers may jump start your business in a new direction. It can be very rewarding to help others while growing your business. You may even find a mentor that can provide you with new ideas you can use.

Baby boomers are even demanding creative funerals. Event planners are now joining forces with the funeral industry. Memorial services are being held on golf courses. Arrangements are being made to have cremations launched into space. Thanks to these innovative companies, people are able to bid farewell their way.

Every form of media is shouting, "Americans are overweight." This negative can turn into a positive growth opportunity for your business. Plus size clothing, even furniture is now being redesigned and is fashionable. Fitness centers (co-ed and woman only) are dotting the landscape. Personal trainers are in demand. Diet meals are being delivered to your door. Fast food restaurants offer salads and fruit as alternatives to French fries. Consumers are reading the nutritional information on labels. More people are concerned about how things are prepared, calorie count, or if it's organic.

Stress is said to lead to obesity. As a result, more people are turning to yoga, hiring personal assistants, seeking help with house cleaning, and even participating in therapy. Carefully consider if this unfortunate trend towards American's obesity can result in opportunities for your business to "fatten its bottom-line."

Are there industry statistics that can give your product or service credibility and attract use by a specific demographic? For example, the International Association of Home Staging reported that when homes are professionally staged for sale and decluttered they sell quicker and for an average of 7% more money. Sharing these statistics with potential customers can make the home seller more likely to hire your services. Almost every business has an association that can provide you with factual statistics.

Doctors and dentists attract their patients by touting that they are specialists. Spotlighting your specialty can bring your targeted demographic knocking at your door. If you are a moving company, is your target customer moving across town, across the state, or across the country? If you are a photographer, do you take photographs at weddings, celebrations, or do you specialize in landscapes? If you are an artist, is your medium oil, watercolors, pottery, or stained glass? If education is your field, do you tutor high school students in a particular course, prepare students to pass standardized tests, or teach a foreign language? Do you run a consignment boutique? If so, do you specialize in brand name items at discount prices, women's clothes, plus sizes, children's items, or furniture? Is your fitness center co-ed or exclusively for woman? Your specialty is your niche. Customers who need what your product or service can provide are your target.

Religious, ethnic guidelines exist regarding the preparation and distribution of some products. You need to understand and respect the cultural values, standards and protocol when targeting such a niche. The Subway Franchise chain has recently opened a kosher sandwich shop in a predominantly Jewish neighborhood in the Flatbush section of Brooklyn. They took note of the demographic of their location and used the information to target a niche. They have tapped into a customer base that previously may not have had the opportunity to eat traditional American-style fast food. Now they have a "Subway" that has adapted its menu and prepared their sandwiches to meet kosher dietary laws.

Safety, fun, a "feels like home" atmosphere, are important features to people choosing day care whether it is for their child, parent, or pet. Post any signs or awards or commendations you have received. It will instill confidence that can result in your facility being selected.

Even if you sell something that has lots of competition you can implement your own personal twist. Wendy's Old Fashioned Hamburgers has created a niche by serving square burgers instead of round ones like the majority of other fast food chains. They used this little difference to create a big marketing statement. Imprinted on each take-out bag it says, "For Wendy's square isn't so much a shape as a promise to not cut corners." What can your company do that will set your products or service apart from your competition?

Never lose sight of your niche markets. Become vigilant in seeking ways to expand your current customer base by exploring new uses for your product or service. Your customers can be your best resource. Targeting specific demographics or multiple niches' can revive your tired sales more quickly and effectively than diluting your effectiveness marketing haphazardly to everyone.

Bounce Back.

Everyone likes "buy one and get one free" specials. Unfortunately, they aren't the best remedy for tired sales and drooping profits. What you want is for customers to buy one and then buy another and another and another. What you need is a "bounce back" marketing strategy that will help you multiply your sales.

"Bounce back" marketing is when you show your appreciation for an initial sale and entice the customer to return. Loyalty programs such as airlines rewarding frequent fliers have gained popularity. You earn credits towards a free flight every time you purchase a ticket on a specific carrier. Hotels reward returning guests with the chance to earn a free stay. Convenience stores, restaurants, car washes, tanning, nail and beauty salons often provide customers with punch cards. After so many purchases, their customers can earn a free beverage, lunch, car wash or discount on a service. Don't make the requirements difficult to reach. Design your program so that participation is easy to track and gives consumers a reason to return and purchase again and again.

Some companies reward their loyal customers with additional discounts. The customer signs up for the reward program. In return they receive special "members only" discount coupons via e-mail or regular mail. People who participate with their local movie theatre reward program can receive a coupon for a free beverage, popcorn or movie. It is a great way to encourage their clientele to view the newest movie release there and not go elsewhere.

Several companies have introduced sophisticated programs that keep track of the amount of money their customer spends during the course of a year. At the end of the year the customer is given a "credit" equal to a predetermined percentage of the money they spent. They can use that credit towards purchases at that business during a preset time for redemption.

Whether you design a program that is based on the distribution of coupons, points, or monetary credit, your goal is to inspire loyalty. We recognize that a specific "loyalty program" isn't always conducive and cost effective for all types of businesses. It is possible, however, for any and all companies to take advantage of some form of "bounce back" marketing.

When you send out your invoice, include a thank you at the bottom with a coupon for a future discount. Most software allows you to automatically add a personalized message to the bottom of your invoice. It is a great place to remind customers of the other products you offer or announce your next sale.

Make it easy for your customers to reorder. If you sell furniture, electronics, food items or offer services that are repeatedly needed such as pet care, plumbing, cleaning, taxes, or printing, be sure to include a sticker, magnet or other item that includes your contact information. When appropriate, attach the information directly to the item so it won't get lost. Otherwise, make sure your contact information will be placed where your customer will view it often. Magnets live on the refrigerator; a calendar with monthly coupons inspires use. There are catalogs filled with promotional items that you can have imprinted and distribute. Keep in mind that you don't want your contact information stuck in a drawer, lost among a sea of other promotional items, commonly referred to as chachkes.

If you have several businesses under one umbrella, or offer various services, or an array of products it is possible to design a "bounce back" strategy that will have a ricochet effect and multiply your sales. For example: If you own a restaurant, you might offer a discount on your catering services. Your customer already knows you prepare delicious food. You "bounce" them to your sister company. If you run a fitness studio and sell equipment, and offer personal training, and apparel, you have several products and services that can cross promote each other. By adding a lounge area where protein shakes and nutritional food supplements are sold, a social atmosphere is established. Customers "bounce back" often and the opportunity for additional sales increases.

Developing "preferred partnerships" is another way to maximize "bounce back" marketing. Airlines have been doing this for years. In addition to earning points when you fly on their planes, they have created partnerships with car rental companies, hotel chains, and cruise lines. Refer back to Chapter 4, *Re-invent the wheel; dare to be a renegade.* Re-read about aligning yourself with partners; it may stimulate your creative juices. Consider what opportunities you have to establish "preferred partnerships."

Don't neglect the opportunity to create a "preferred partnership" with your suppliers. If you are a landscaper, partner with the business where you get your flowers, shrubs and supplies. They will recommend your services to their customers who want to hire a landscaper. In return you "bounce back" and purchase your gardening supplies from them. They "bounce" more customers in your direction and you continue to "bounce back" to purchase from them.

If you have a website, you need to make customers not only "stick" when they visit but "bounce back" often. Give them a reason to return. When possible and appropriate, incorporate interactive games, videos, and message boards to get visitors involved and anxious to return. Keep your information current. Don't leave it unchanged for more than a few days, a week at most. If the information is stale, eyeballs will go elsewhere. Provide an "opt-in" option so they may receive special offers, a newsletter, and notification of upcoming seminars and new products. To help eliminate being thought of as a "spammer;" ask new subscribers to respond to an e-mail that confirms their interest.

Consider participating in Affiliate Programs. This lets other sites promote your products or services in return for a commission on any sales they generate. Building mutually beneficial relationships can lead to links between other company's websites and yours. This can dramatically multiply the number of clicks you receive. Increased visibility means increased sales potential.

When developing your "bounce back" strategy you want to ask yourself two questions. What would motivate the customer to make their next purchase sooner rather than later? How can we say thank you that is both cost effective and instills customer loyalty? The best incentive for customers to "bounce back" and purchase again and again is to provide a quality product, and create a positive customer experience at an affordable price.

Build a galaxy of customers.

As a consumer, it isn't likely that you remember everything you've ever purchased and from where. On the other hand, you may remember those instances when you had an extraordinarily good or disastrous experience. You remember the online shopping experiences that made you feel safe when submitting your personal information. You return to do business with those companies that delivered on their promises and made it easy and convenient for you to purchase.

When a family member, friend or colleague asks where you purchased an item, you probably included your editorial opinion regarding your experience as well as answering their question. It is human nature to share our opinions. You want your customers to give a positive review of their shopping experience with your company.

Satisfied customers are your most valuable marketing resource. "Word-of-mouth" advertising has the power to destroy your business or catapult it to levels of success beyond what you may have imagined. You want to recruit your customers to become active members of your sales force.

Studies show that after two years, approximately 70% of most companies' business is repeat or the result of referrals. This statistic illustrates the importance of building relationships with your customers. You need to develop the "likeability factor" and instill a sense of confidence, trust, and reliability in your product or service.

You never know who your customer will have lunch with, join in a round of golf, or talk to tomorrow. Everyone is the center of their own sphere of influence. They represent the center of a star. The rays are the people that touch their lives. For example: One of your satisfied customers may have contact with their family, friends, colleagues at work, members of their church, associates in clubs and organizations, their doctor, dentist, lawyer, members of the same gym, their nail technician, beautician, masseuse, pharmacist, etc., etc. You get the idea. Every one of your customers has the potential to tell a wide assortment of people about your company, your product and your service.

Referrals are a great way to build a galaxy of customers. They are an extremely valuable resource, one that is all too often overlooked. You want to get referrals whenever possible.

The best time to ask for a referral is immediately after you have done something that especially pleased your customer or when they felt the experience was particularly rewarding. Your customer will be more responsive after a positive experience. You might want to give your most "influential" customers some of your business cards to distribute to the people they know who might benefit from your product or service. You may even incentify them for each referral they provide.

A referral is an introduction. Ask permission to use your client's name when you talk to the referral. If you get permission to mention your existing client's name, that's great. Having a friend or colleague in common may break the ice with the prospect. Whenever a sale results from a referral, be sure to say, "thank you" for the lead.

It takes time to feel comfortable asking for referrals. People fear rejection or that a Pandora's Box filled with complaints may tumble forth. The more you do it, the less awkward you will feel.

Bill Gates once said, "The most powerful words you can use in asking for referrals are, "I need your help." If you've served your customer, referral, alliance, or prospect well, if you've built rapport and trust, then he or she will be happy to give referrals. You just have to ask."

People don't have a lot of time to shop around. They don't want to take risks. It is easier to make the decision to purchase based on a recommendation than to invest the time to research.

Being the best is "subjective;" the customer decides. People listen to "influencers." They are the people who know which restaurant is "in." They are anxious to determine what is "best" and tell family, friends, and colleagues about the products and services they like or don't like. It doesn't matter if you are the best qualified. The consumer determines what's best for "them" based on their preferences and criteria

You want to learn what your customer's opinion is of your product or service. Google your business. Scan the search engines for information about your company. You need to know what others are saying about your business. It's an important marketing practice. Post your own comments and respond professionally to both praise and concerns. Take advantage of opportunities to join in the conversation and update readers about your products or services. Favorable mention by customers familiar with your product or service can create a positive buzz that can result in new customers.

To thrive as a successful growing business you need to be dedicated to connecting with your customers. The opportunity for the next sale begins immediately following the first sale. It isn't enough to provide a quality product or service that benefits the customer and meets their needs. It isn't enough to make it convenient and easy for them to make a purchase. It isn't enough to create a positive customer experience. You need to develop on-going relationships with your customers.

In this age of self-service and online shopping, you may never have face to face contact with your customers. Thanks to direct mail, incentive programs, signage and the evolving world of Web 2.0, there is still an unlimited potential for connecting with prospects and customers.

Begin by saying, "Thank you" for the sale. Show customers that you recognize they had a choice and that you value their business. Investing the time and energy to learn about your customer and their preferences will pay off with repeat sales opportunities. It may also inspire customers to refer your business to their family, friends and colleagues.

You need to gather information about your customers while being ever cognizant that people don't want to be subjected to the third degree. Instead of asking them to answer a myriad of questions or fill out a questionnaire, give your customers the chance to sign up for a drawing, notification of specials, or to be added to your mailing list. There needs to be an incentive. It goes back to the need to tune into **WIIFM** (**W**hat's **I**n **I**t **F**or **M**e). Your customers are more likely to provide you the information you require if you make it beneficial for them. While trying to elicit the desired information you need, take care that the experience doesn't become an unpleasant one for your customer.

Become a detective. Customers are turned off when they are inundated with questions. They carefully guard their privacy and don't wish to give away their valuable time. It is up to you to take note of a consumer's buying trend. Did they purchase a gift for a special occasion? Do they consistently purchase the same items or use your service at the same time each month? The more you learn about your customer the easier it will be to entice them to purchase again and enlist them as a means to promote your business.

While sharing personal information may make a customer hesitant, most are eager to give feedback. The Internet provides unprecedented opportunities for customers to share their opinions. Encourage your customers to share their thoughts, suggestions, and their ideas for additional uses for your products and services. Listen to what your customers have to say. Let them know their opinions matter. Reward them for their input.

It is possible to build an ever growing galaxy of new customers by reaching out to the "stars" of your business, your current customers. Their recommendations are more powerful than any other marketing strategy. Their influence reaches within their homes and extends into cyberspace. You don't need a doctor to cure your "Tired Sales" and "Drooping Profits." You need customers that will purchase again and again and prescribe your product and service to everyone they know.

Be environmentally conscious.

Environmental responsibility is a hot topic. Being eco-conscious isn't only good for our environment; it can be good for business too. It isn't a coincidence that three of the most admired companies in 2007, GE, Starbucks and Toyota, are each growing their business based on programs designed to help preserve our planet.

Numerous businesses are jumping on the bandwagon to make their companies more environmentally friendly, as well as contributing to much needed research. For example, UPS is increasing its fleet of alternative fueled delivery trucks. British billionaire and entrepreneur, Sir Richard Branson, has pledged that over the next ten years he will donate the profits from the transportation sector of his businesses to the research and development of renewable and alternative energy sources. It is estimated that the profits from his companies, Virgin Atlantic Airlines and Virgin Trains, will result in a donation of approximately $3 billion dollars.

On February 9, 2007 Sir Richard Branson joined former Vice President, Al Gore, to announce the "Virgin Earth Challenge." A Global Science and Technology Prize of $25 million dollars will be awarded to the individual or group that submits the most commercially viable idea that results in the removal of anthropogenic atmospheric greenhouse gases each year for 10 years. There must be no harmful effects and the idea must contribute to the stability of the earth's climate. A panel of judges will oversee the entries including NASA Scientist, James Hansen.

Of course, if you have a solution, please submit your idea. The award will significantly improve your bottom-line. If however, that isn't your area of expertise there are still many ways that going "Green" can provide opportunities for your business to save money and increase your customer base.

If your company is taking initiatives to save our environment, don't keep it a secret. Promote it. Customers have lots of choices today. They want to do business with companies that share their values. Knowing "how" you do business can inspire customers to choose you.

Check into the incentives your state and local utility companies offer. Some utility companies provide free energy audits. It may be possible that by implementing some simple changes you can save money. Consider installing fluorescent lights; motion sensors can turn them on and off to eliminate needless lighting of spaces not used fulltime. Using timers on your sprinklers or installing low flow fixtures can save water. In 2005 more than $12 billion dollars was saved when Energy Star-Certified Products were used in businesses here in the United States. To find a listing of the Energy Efficiency and Renewable Energy Programs in your state, go to the U.S. Department of Energy site at www.eere.energy.gov

Consider participating in your local Earth Day Celebration. This will give you an audience with potential customers who value conservation. Interacting with other eco-conscious business owners may lead to opportunities to work in tandem with your community and other business leaders of like minds. Every facet of your life can lead to ideas that may save money and increase your company's visibility and sales base.

Toot your own horn.

People need to be aware of your business before they can purchase from you or suggest your products or service. In previous chapters we have discussed the importance of submitting press releases, volunteering, sponsoring teams, and charity events, as well as becoming active in neighborhood business associations. To help your company thrive you need to make sure people know that your business exists.

You need to fight any introverted tendencies you may have. It is up to you to use the contacts you have to grow your business. Networking doesn't mean boring everyone by talking about yourself. Instead you can build clientele by finding ways to make stories about your business interesting. Stress how your product and/or service fills needs and offers benefits. Don't wait until you are desperate for business to start talking about your products or service.

A popular way to "toot your own horn" and keep customers and prospects informed about your business is to develop and distribute a newsletter. It can be beneficial and provide a compliment to your other advertising and marketing activities. A newsletter can build awareness of your company, products and services.

Before you automatically jump on the newsletter bandwagon, there are some things to consider. How much will it cost to produce and distribute? Will your newsletter be published in print format, electronically, or both? Do you have the necessary software? How often will a new issue be published; daily, weekly, monthly or quarterly? Do you have the time and expertise to create and maintain the newsletter or will you need to hire out the responsibility? How will you get your newsletter viewed by past, present and potential customers?

A newsletter can be a powerful marketing tool; however, it must be read to be effective. There must be something about your newsletter that gives it a perceived value. It can be educational and informative. You can use it to share tips, a calendar of upcoming events, and to introduce new products or services. Include testimonials and photos of customers who have enjoyed and benefited from your goods and services. Provide coupons and offer special discounts to subscribers.

Keep your newsletter brief as well as beneficial. People don't have the time or desire to read long articles. They prefer tidbits of information they can use and digest quickly. Proofread your copy to make sure that nothing inadvertently offends anyone. Make it easy for subscribers to sign up their family, friends and colleagues. You want to increase and maximize circulation.

Carefully consider your answers to the questions we've asked before investing the time and expense of adding a newsletter to your marketing plan. Your decision should be based on evaluating costs (both money and time) versus your return on the investment. If you decide there is value in proceeding, make a specific goal oriented plan.

Keep in mind that there are many companies anxious to help you with this project. Shop and compare if you decide to outsource. There are also assortments of software packages available if you decide to tackle this on your own. Although creating a newsletter can require a lot of time and energy to develop, it can be a valuable way to establish a credible presence with your customers.

Signage is also an excellent way to "toot your horn" and spread your message. There are lots of different opportunities to advertise via signs. There are billboards, yard signs, banners, notice boards, signs inside and outside your location, sandwich boards, and signage at ballgames and events. There are even signs pulled behind planes or written in the sky. You have lots of choices. They run the gamut in price. One kind or another can fit into your budget.

If you are in construction, do landscaping, or install pools, yard signs are a terrific way to showcase your work. Candidates have been using them for years to serve as non-verbal testimonials and encourage people to vote for them. Plumbers and electricians have had equal success utilizing yard signs to announce that they were selected to do the job. Be sure to include your contact information in bold, easy to read print. If you offer "free estimates" or guarantee your work, include that on your sign.

Promote your business by showing off your logo. It is the flag of your brand. You can emblaze it on anything, everything. T-shirts and hats with an imprint of your logo can serve as uniforms to identify your staff to your customers. They can become a source of additional income if you sell them. Anytime a customer is wearing your logo hat or shirt or carrying a tote with you logo printed on it, they are advertising your company. Wear your logo; write with a pen sporting your logo, you might even drive a vehicle sporting your logo. Always have business cards available and ready to be handed out.

If your employees are specialists or have earned designations that set them apart from your competition spotlight them. For example if you own a company that services automobiles and your staff is "certified in auto repair" advertise it. These technicians can provide a competitive edge. Consider offering workshops to educate potential clients about preparing their cars for winter, hurricane car care, or what every woman needs to know. As an incentive, consider offering an award for participation in any seminars you offer.

Showcase the expertise your company offers in workshops, online seminars, podcasts, videos, and in your newsletter. Become the source newspapers and talk radio hosts turn to for an informed point of view. Your reputation as an authority will create a sense of confidence in customers that will result in sales.

Visit your local party store. It is filled with items you can use to draw attention to your location. A bubble machine might be the perfect attention-getter for a Laundromat.

Brightly colored balloons, or themed decorations, or life size cardboard cut-outs of celebrities may provide the perfect little something that will motivate customers to stop and visit your business. Use them to draw attention and add an element of fun. Never use them to mislead customers that you have a celebrity's endorsement.

Place your advertising where time slows to a crawl. Hospitals and waiting areas are perfect places to put copies of your newsletter. Specialty publications that are found in these areas (such as hospital newsletters, and publications targeting children, families and seniors) are always looking for articles as well as offer inexpensive advertising opportunities. Visit the places in your community where people are searching for something to read while they wait. Pick up copies of the complimentary publications and investigate if there is an affordable opportunity for you to promote your products or services.

Use e-mail to reach your audience. It is inexpensive and immediate. The results can easily be tracked. A recipient will decide to open an e-mail in less than five seconds. The subject line is the key. State the benefit you offer in fifty characters or less. Make sure the content is relevant to the customer.

Showcase your reviews, endorsements and awards. Post them on your site. Display them at your location. Feature them in your promotional materials. Get the word out and let prospects and customers know about your success.

It is your obligation to keep your message in front of your customers and prospects. Consumers can be fickle and have a short memory. It is your responsibility to make sure they don't forget your company. They need to be reminded of the value and benefits your products and services provide. Don't be shy. If you want to increase your sales it is up to you to "Toot your own horn."

Chapter 9

◆

You and your business can make a difference.

Inevitably, once your business gains exposure you will find yourself inundated with requests for donations, sponsorships and participation in charitable events. You may feel like a piece of meat being attacked by piranha or you may find yourself wanting to do it all. Thousands of opportunities exist for you to make a positive difference. Savvy businesses are selective. They recognize that they can't afford to contribute to everything. They need to choose.

It is important to give careful consideration to your options before you decide. You want to support the issues you care about and those that align well with your business.

I hear you saying, "How can I donate when I barely make enough to cover expenses?" Many small businesses don't have the discretionary funds available to give substantial amounts of money to any non-profit organization or charity. You may have the desire but unfortunately the profits aren't there yet. Contributing money isn't the only way you can make a difference.

Bill Gates, Warren Buffet, and Oprah are in the headlines; each is famous for their philanthropy. It may surprise you but it isn't their financial contributions that are responsible for making the biggest difference. It is their ability to encourage and inspire others to join their efforts that makes them valuable instruments improving the "status quo" and making things better.

You don't have to wait. You can get involved now and make a positive difference while at the same time grow your business. The more you make, the more you can share.

"If you think you are too small to be effective, you have never been in bed with a mosquito." Betty Reese, Pilot

It is said that in 1939 when Hewlett-Packard started its company, they only had $538.00 to back their venture. Even so, the company donated $5 to the Salvation Army that year. During the fiscal year, 2005, it is reported that HP contributed over $45 million to organizations worldwide. They focus their philanthropic donations and partnerships in the areas of education, community and employee giving.

Aligning your company with a cause or non-profit organization can create win-win marketing. Your customers will have additional reasons to feel good about purchasing your product or service. It can build customer and employee loyalty. Your business gains a reputation for caring and depending on the campaign, increased visibility and sales can results.

Don't feel self-conscious about profiting from a marketing strategy that includes partnering with charitable organizations. Actor Paul Newman based his entire venture into the food business on the principle of helping others. Since the inception of his "Newman's Own" line of food items, over \$100 million has been donated to organizations around the world.

Deciding how to become involved depends on what you sell and who you are targeting as potential customers. Obviously, if your business promotes the vegan lifestyle you don't want to volunteer to collect turkeys for holiday distribution. You want to make sure the cause you support is in tune with your beliefs and corporate goals. You want to choose something that resonates with you, your community, and customers.

It doesn't take millions of dollars to facilitate change. It takes desire and commitment. The following are ways your business can make a difference without draining your bank account. We hope these ideas will jump start your creative imagination and with a little customizing you will integrate them into your overall business strategy.

Share your location.

Whether your business is in a building, storefront or located in cyberspace, you can use it to spotlight issues and concerns. Allow organizations the opportunity to post signage promoting their cause. Advertise upcoming charitable events. Even allowing someone to use your location to post a "Lost & Found" picture to help a family find their lost pet shows you care.

If you have an actual "physical location," consider using it as a drop off point. Lots of charities are looking for collection points; Toys for Tots, food for the hungry, clothing for the needy to name just a few. Permit schools, clubs or organizations to use your location as a site for their fundraising bake sale or car wash. Give carte blanche for Girl Scouts to sell their cookies, or the Red Cross to set-up their truck for blood donations. If you have meeting space or a conference room, you might offer it to committees, clubs or organizations that need a place to meet.

Radio remotes are not only sales based; many support causes. Invite the station to broadcast from your store or business. When people come to make a contribution or see the radio celebrities, they will be visiting your location. Every visitor is a potential customer.

In this age of online videos and podcasts, it is possible for you to showcase a charity event or educate the public about an issue via your website. Providing a resource that illuminates a concern or cause can be a catalyst that ultimately increases monetary contributions.

Use your "location," whether it is made of brick and mortar or online, to help your community and to promote goodwill. Contributing space and the opportunity for signage provides a helping hand. It can be as valuable as writing a check. In return for sharing your location, the non-profit organization, charity or cause will benefit. You will attract visitors to your store or site, visitors that one day may become your customers.

Share the proceeds.

Select a cause or issue to support that is close to your heart. Ask your employees, neighbors, and family for ideas. You may decide to support one charity, or perhaps you will decide to lend your support to a different cause each month. You need to decide what best fits your values and provides you the best opportunity to help.

There are several ways you can share your proceeds and not invest more than you can afford. Select a particular product or service and designate a percentage of its sales to be donated. Instead of targeting a particular item, you may choose one day a month when a percentage of the proceeds from that day's sales will be donated. In lieu of a percentage, you can establish a specific amount; for example if you own a florist, a $1 could be donated to All Children's Hospital for every bouquet that is ordered for Mother's Day.

You can share your proceeds in helpful, creative ways without giving away hard dollars. For example, if you operate a dry cleaner you might offer to give a coupon for $5 worth of free dry cleaning to anyone who drops off a suit to donate to charity. After these suits are cleaned, they can be given to the local charity in your community that is helping the underprivileged and unemployed find a job. You are supporting a worthy organization. You are helping others gain confidence when they go for their job interview. At the same time you are perpetuating additional sales from your customer who has been awarded the coupon for their generosity.

Many businesses are providing schools, charities and non-profit organizations with coupons they can sell. The coupons provide the buyer with discounts on the product or service offered. Auto repair shops, beauty salons, movies, restaurants, fitness centers and spa services have found these coupons work well. The school or organization receives the total cost of the coupon, usually $5, $10 or $20. The customer presents their coupon at the participating business and receives that amount in discount. The business gets new customers and only reduces the cost of their product or service when the coupon is redeemed.

Before you become involved with any promotions or donations, verify the regulations. It is important to include disclaimers that explain the program. Be clear that the documents have no cash value and aren't valid if duplicated.

Use your imagination and create special packages or incentives that can be sold and promoted as a means of raising funds for your designated cause. For example, in an effort to fight Aids several companies have joined forces to sell "Product (Red)." T-shirts and various clothing is available at the Gap. Converse is also involved and there is even a special edition iPod. You might join in such a campaign or create your own.

For example: If you sell children's apparel, you might establish a program that provides support to your local zoo. Every time someone purchases a stuffed animal, a donation is made to the zoo. If you are a real estate agent you might offer to give a percentage of your commission to Habitat for Humanity. Customize a program that works for you.

It is crucial to promote your programs. Submit press releases to the newspaper. Share details of your programs on your site, on signage in your store, and in your newsletter and advertising. You want to give people the opportunity to purchase the products and services they need while partnering with you to make a positive difference.

Get involved, volunteer, participate.

Often it is time that is rarer than money. Some people would prefer to give money and be done with it. Money alone isn't enough. It is important to get involved.

Volunteer to participate on Boards and Advisory Committees for non-profit and community based organizations. Share your time and develop a relationship. Monetary contributions may follow but start by becoming involved. Non-profits and community based committees are very interested in utilizing business expertise when setting the course for their organization and helping them work more effectively.

Offer to serve on the planning committee for the annual dinner or for a special event. You will make a positive contribution without necessarily making a lengthy commitment. Along the way, you will likely establish new friendships and relationships that may benefit your business in ways that you can only imagine. A note of caution, don't "work the room" too much looking for leads. Remember you are there to help support the organization and/or cause, which is another reason to select a cause that means something to you.

Harley-Davidson has long been active supporting various causes and organizations. They believe that it is equally, if not more important, to be visible and show your support. They encourage their employees to participate in bike rallies and volunteer at charity events.

Do you or your employees, walk, run or bike? If so, consider participating in one or more of the local races held in support of your charity of choice.

If physical exercise isn't your cup of tea, you can still participate as a volunteer. You can point people in the right direction along the route, pass out water, or help with registration. Events are always looking for volunteers. It is a great chance to get involved and also network.

Man the phones for a telethon, serve food, wash dishes, deliver items; your goal is to help. Depending on your budget, you might volunteer to do the printing for an event, distribute flyers, sell tickets, and help decorate the venue or provide chair massages to the weary workers. Your contribution doesn't need to be expensive or time consuming to be valuable.

Sponsor

Often when a business hears "sponsor" the first thing that comes to mind is athletic teams. You pay for team shirts and/or hats that have your name and logo emblazoned across them. This can be a terrific way to increase your visibility *but* it can be costly. It may initially be more affordable to purchase space in the yearbook or buy advertising in the outfield; all are ways to sponsor a team.

There are other ways to become involved with sponsorship beyond sports. You can support and sponsor a cause by purchasing a license plate that contributes its revenue to your cause. Many states have a wide variety of plates available. They support college teams, causes like preventing domestic abuse, to supporting the police and fire departments.

Students may need financial help to participate in a contest, field trips or educational travel abroad. Your business may be able to donate funds to make their trips a reality. If you don't have funds, you may be able to donate items or services that can be auctioned to raise money. You don't have to act alone to make a difference. Team up with other businesses, civic organizations and clubs. Together you may be able to provide scholarships, assist with the building of a community center, or sponsor programs that recognize activists in the areas of energy conservation, education, and preserving the environment.

Consider giving teenagers the opportunity to intern at your company. Providing an opportunity for them to learn about business first hand can provide a priceless learning experience regardless of your product or service. Check with your local school system, Boys and Girls Club and YMCA/YWCA for opportunities to get involved and contribute to today's youth. You would be a valued mentor.

Interns can bring a fresh and youthful perspective to your business. Harness their creative powers and insight. At the heart of any good internship program, participants should have the opportunity to learn and be inspired to make contributions. Another alternative to a full-time intern is to participate in the annual National "Ground Hog Job Shadow Day." Students across the country get the opportunity to shadow career mentors and learn what various jobs require. This program is usually sponsored by the local Chamber of Commerce. For details enter: http://www.jobshadow.org/. Getting involved in this program contributes to the student's education and provides you networking opportunities with other business leaders in the community.

Lend a helping hand.

The number of programs available to participate in is staggering. Whether your allegiance is to our men and women in the military and our veterans, animal rights, finding a cure, assisting the less fortunate, or stopping injustice, there is a program you can join and support. If you don't want to join an established group, you can pave your own path to help.

Offer discounts to members of the military and their families. Volunteer at your local SPCA. Create your own t-shirts to raise money to donate towards researching a cure. Collect food and clothing for those in need. Stomp out injustice by showing goodwill to others.

Sometimes Mother Nature, fire, illness and death invade our lives and become newsworthy emergencies. Be ready to come to the aid of those in need. You'd be surprised how little you have to do in order to make a huge positive difference.

"I've learned that you shouldn't go through life with a catcher's mitt on both hands. You need to be able to throw something back." Maya Angelou, poet and author

Integrate "Cause Marketing" into your marketing strategy. Choose a cause that means something to you, that you can passionately support. Track your success. Don't be self conscious; use PR to share details of your efforts. Your ideas may inspire others and have a contagious effect. Being socially responsible is good for business and benefits society. You can make a difference.

Chapter 10

◆

"I'll do it someday."
Hmm, where is someday on the calendar?

We hope this book has boosted your innovation quotient. That the questions were provocative, giving you reason to review and ponder your current strategies and inspire you to redirect your focus and take action.

You need to concentrate your efforts on those tasks that will best contribute to maximizing your visibility, sales and profitability. Identify "what needs to be done;" that is more important than limiting your efforts to "what you want to do."

You want to customize a "strategy" that will work for YOUR business. It isn't necessary to do everything at once. Incremental enhancements to your current marketing and sales plan will launch you in the right direction. Don't waste your time and energy with thoughts of "if only" I'd thought of this or done that before now.

Let go of habits and negative thoughts that drain your energy. Instead use your fears, past mistakes, and frustrations to fuel your energy and commitment to achieve success. Regret no yesterdays, they'll be another one here tomorrow. Instead move forward to devise a plan that will create an atmosphere that promotes thriving, not merely surviving.

Alice in Wonderland asked the Cheshire Cat, "Would you tell me please, which way I ought to go from here?" He replied, "That depends a good deal on where you want to get to." That is exactly what you need to determine. Where do you want to go from here? The future is becoming the present at turbo speed. Now is the time to use the answers you've given to the multitude of questions in this book and determine what the goals for your business are.

In the battle of action versus intention, all too often, intention wins out. Naysayers tell you, "It can't be done." Inertia sets in. You get busy maintaining the "status quo." You have the best of intentions but there is never enough time.

Remember, "You have exactly the same number of hours per day that were given to Pasteur, Michelangelo, Mother Teresa, Helen Keller, Leonardo da Vinci, Thomas Jefferson, and Albert Einstein." H. Jackson Brown, Jr. author of *Life's Little Instruction Book.*

Don't allow self defeating thoughts, time management challenges, or doomsday prognostications to stop you from pursuing your goals. Nothing relieves the sting of criticism from disapproving skeptics as much as success. Dream big and focus on the small details everyday. Never be afraid to challenge yourself. Believe in your passion; it is your company's most valuable asset.

You may wish to seek advice from someone else that has already paved a similar path to profitability and been successful. Don't let titles, status or reputation stop you from seeking counsel from the best. You might be surprised how readily they respond and offer to help. It is YOUR business and although it is helpful to seek advice from others there is nothing wrong with "doing it your way."

Create a specific strategy based upon your unique products or services. Give careful consideration to the demographics and needs of your customers. Throwing everything against the wall and hoping something will stick only leads to a messy wall.

"Strategy" is defined as a plan of action designed to achieve a particular goal. Dan Miller, author and personal life coach offers this example, "Imagine you are driving in a Corvette at 80 mph headed toward Los Angeles but you really want to go to Nashville. Accelerating to 120 mph may give you the sense that you are really making progress, temporarily. But what you actually need to do is change direction." Is your current strategy working? Don't be afraid to change direction.

Visualize your goals. Establish a timeline; it may need to be adjusted but having a timeline for action will keep you focused. Evaluate and track your progress. This is crucial. You don't want stubbornness to keep you headed in the wrong direction or invested in an unprofitable strategy. If one plan fails, back-up. Convert failure and disappointment into a learning experience. Many people give up when one last try would mean success. The solution may be just a day away.

Don't fall victim to the misguided belief that unless you spend a lot of money or aren't as creative as DaVinci you won't succeed. Some people wouldn't even try if they were given a 100% guarantee of success.

Business success requires vision, focus, leadership, discipline and execution, an incredible work ethic, confidence and the drive to achieve. It is time for you to create a plausible vision. As Sherlock Holmes said, "Break away from the status quo execute at low cost, uncomplicated practical ways to chart a path to profitability."

Believe in yourself, your business, your product, and your service. It is time to take things off the "back burner." Once the momentum begins, don't pause, doubts may creep in. Find the methods that best relate your product or service to your customer. Take calculated risks and rebound from setbacks. In today's business environment there are unprecedented opportunities for dynamic growth.

We have given you ideas designed to jump-start your own imagination. We have shared quotes, examples and insights from well respected people who have let nothing stand in the way of achieving their goals. We appreciate that you invested the time to read this book. Now it is your choice how you use it.

Refuse to limit yourself. Accept the inevitability of change. Expect and embrace it rather than fear it. Give yourself permission to succeed beyond your wildest expectations.

Life is filled with phenomenal possibilities. This is one of the most exciting times in our history. Trust your instincts. Be proud of what you've accomplished, continue. Renew your enthusiasm, revitalize your dream. The best way to have a fantastic future is to invent it.

This is YOUR "someday."

We hope that you have discovered ideas that you will use or adapt to increase your visibility, sales and profits.

We would love to hear about your successes, ideas and suggestions so they can be passed along to inspire other entrepreneurs.

Your, "Oops, I wish I hadn't done that" are also welcome. They may help others avoid following in your footprints.

E-mail your ideas to Mzdavinci@aol.com

Please write "Ideas" in the subject line. We will spotlight them on http://mzdavinci.com

About the Author

Judy McKay has more than 20 years of experience in both sales and marketing. She is currently the CEO and Creative Director of Ideas Unlimited. Judy customizes strategic action plans that will increase sales and profitability. Her goal is to inspire and provide ideas that will help you achieve success.

978-0-595-46127-1
0-595-46127-1

www.ingramcontent.com/pod-product-compliance
Lightning Source LLC
Chambersburg PA
CBHW030840180526
45163CB00004B/1399